Another Twenty Five Favourite Walks in Surrey, Sussex and Hampshire

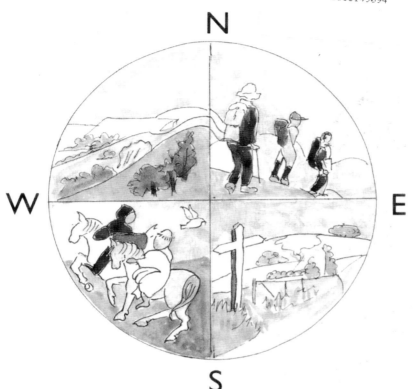

This book has been compiled by members of the Godalming and Haslemere Group of the Ramblers' Association and offers 25 walks over a wide area from north of Guildford to the Sussex Coast, and Alresford in Hampshire to the South Downs, north of Brighton. As many of the walks offer longer and shorter versions, more than 50 different options are described.

Front cover: Drawing by Len Cook. Photograph by Julian Yorke. View towards Black Down from Limbo near Petworth – see walk 18.

Sketch maps by Julian Yorke and Robert Adam; area maps by Ray Pont; illustrations by Jane House; compiled and edited by Monica Long.

Printed 2008

Foreword

This book is a compilation of another twenty five favourite walks in Surrey, Sussex and Hampshire, written by members of the Godalming and Haslemere Group of the Ramblers' Association, people who know and love the area. Many of the walks offer more than one version so there is plenty of choice.

The production of this book has been a tremendous group effort using the talents of many people. Members have checked and double checked every walk to ensure that you can go out and walk with confidence. We have been fortunate to have members who have drawn the sketches, plotted the maps and designed the cover. We hope that this enthusiasm, care and attention to detail will help you to enjoy walking in this lovely part of southern England.

We would like to thank Blackdown Press Ltd., for all their technical advice and support during the development of the book. We are also grateful to Blackdown Press Ltd., Ramblers Holidays Ltd. and Breaking Free for their generous support in advertising.

We do hope you enjoy the walks in this book, and if you do not already have a copy of our original book 'Twenty Five Favourite Walks in West Surrey and Sussex' you might like to buy it too. To order, please see the details on page 5.

The Ramblers' Association

The Ramblers' Association is dedicated to:

Promoting walking for everyone as a healthy, fun and inexpensive activity.
Safeguarding the countryside from unsightly and polluting developments.
Increasing opportunities for responsible access for everyone.
Protecting Britain's unique network of public paths.
Providing walking information and educating walkers about their rights and responsibilities.
For more details, and to join, contact **www.ramblers.org.uk** or The Ramblers' Association, 2nd Floor, Camelford House, 87-90 Albert Embankment, London, SE1 7TW.
Telephone: 020 7339 8500

The Godalming and Haslemere Group was established in 1974, and has over 430 members. We have an extensive walks programme led by members of the group; details are available on **www.godalmingandhaslemere.org.uk** or in the local press. In addition to our walks programme we have a varied range of social activities including group holidays and coach rambles. We also have a volunteer working party which during the summer assists with the maintenance of the local rights of way network. We are always pleased to welcome new people on our walks and hope you will join the Ramblers' Association and walk with us.

Contents

Contents

Contents

British Library Cataloguing in Publication Data.
A catalogue record of this book is available from the British Library.

ISBN 1 901184 81 1

© *Godalming and Haslemere Group of the Ramblers' Association*

Copies of this book are obtainable from: **www.godalmingandhaslemereramblers.org.uk.**

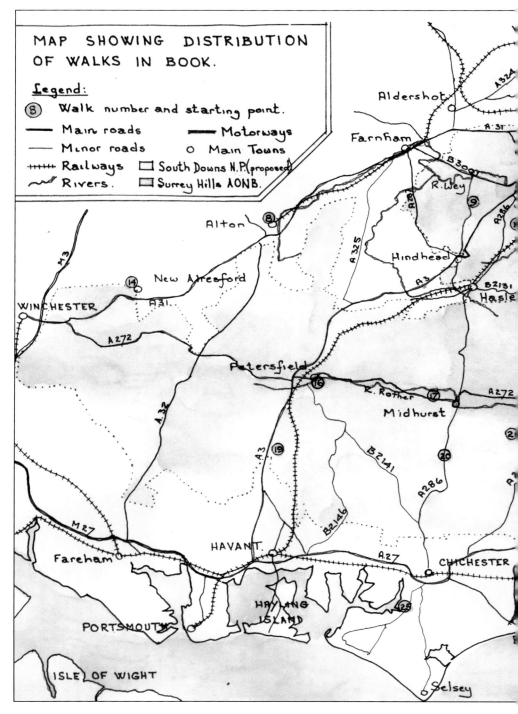

MAP SHOWING DISTRIBUTION
OF WALKS IN BOOK.

Legend:
- (8) Walk number and starting point.
- —— Main roads
- —— Minor roads
- +++++ Railways
- ~~ Rivers.
- ▬▬ Motorways
- O Main Towns
- ☐ South Downs N.P.(proposed)
- ☐ Surrey Hills AONB.

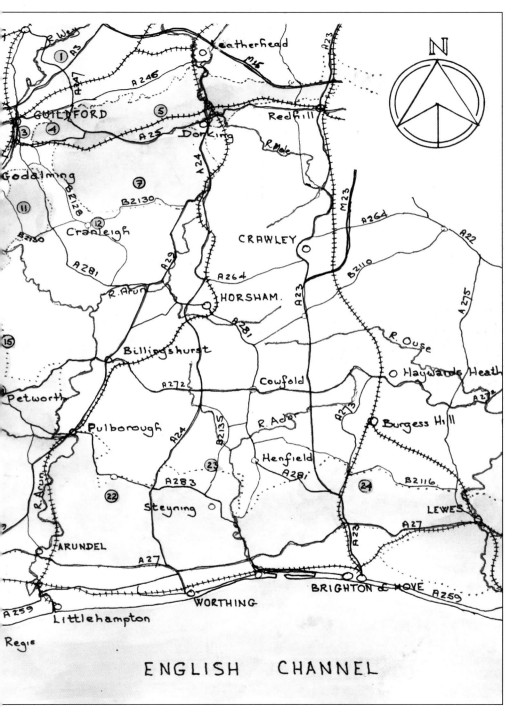

Notes for Users

The majority of walks are circular and are often planned to include a pub stop or a favourite picnic place around the halfway stage. The information at the start of each walk gives details of all refreshment stops along the way. Do check the sketch map for their positions along the route. The information given is correct at the time of publication and does not imply any particular recommendation. Some walks also point out places of interest along the way.

The maps referred to are the Ordnance Survey (OS) Landranger series 1:50,000 (2cm to 1km/1¼inches to 1mile), and the Explorer series 1:25,000 (4cm to 1 km/2½inches to 1mile). Both show public rights of way, and open access land is included in the newer versions of the Explorer series. The Explorer series is designed for walkers and includes field boundaries and other helpful details. An OS grid reference (GR) is given to locate the start of each walk and applies to either map.

The section numbers in the walk descriptions relate to those on the sketch maps and we have aimed to make the two together sufficient for you to find your way. However, it is always best to have a map handy and a compass can also be useful on heaths and commons to check your direction.

Distances are given in kilometres/metres as well as miles/yards. The lengths given for the walks have all been measured from Explorer maps and are an indication only. They may differ from measurements taken via GPS or pedometer, particularly on hilly ground.

As the RA encourages the use of public transport, links are outlined where appropriate but as services are variable they should be checked before setting out.

National Rail Enquiries   Tel: 0845 748 4950
Traveline (bus enquiries)   Tel: 0871 200 2233

Transport Direct (journey planner):   www.transportdirect.info

The routes described use rights of way or other paths open to the public wherever possible. Over time some paths may be legally diverted or extinguished, so please remember that small changes of route may become necessary. These should be clearly signed by the County Council.

While the walk descriptions are accurate at the time of going to press it is inevitable that changes will occur; for example many stiles in these counties are being replaced by kissing gates, trees can be cut down or heathland cleared.

Obstructions to rights of way should be reported to The Ramblers' Association, 2nd Floor, Camelford House, 87-90 Albert Embankment, London, SE1 7TW, who will inform the appropriate local representative.

Lastly, please ensure you have the appropriate clothing, footwear, and equipment for the prevailing weather.

Enjoy your walking!

The Countryside Code for the public

Helping everyone to respect, protect and enjoy our countryside

Be Safe – plan ahead and follow any signs. Follow advice and local signs, and be prepared for the unexpected.

Leave gates and property as you find them – please respect the working life of the countryside.

Protect plants and animals, and take your litter home – make sure you don't harm animals, birds, plants or trees.

Keep dogs under close control – it's every owner's duty to make sure their dog is not a danger or a nuisance to other animals, wildlife or other people.

Consider other people – showing consideration and respect for other people makes the countryside a pleasant environment for everyone.

1 Walking beside the waters: river, canal, ponds and lakes - Ripley, Wisley and the River Wey Navigation

Peter A's walk

Length: 15¼km/9½miles (sections 1-5, 7-11) with a shorter version of 7km/4½miles (sections 1, 2, 4-6).

Maps: OS Landranger 186; Explorer 145.

Start: GR 053571 Ripley Green. From Ripley High Street (B2215) turn onto the metalled track leading across the green to Dunsborough Farm (beware speed bumps). Ignore the car park on your right and continue to the parking area on the left between the cricket ground on your right and the children's play area on your left.

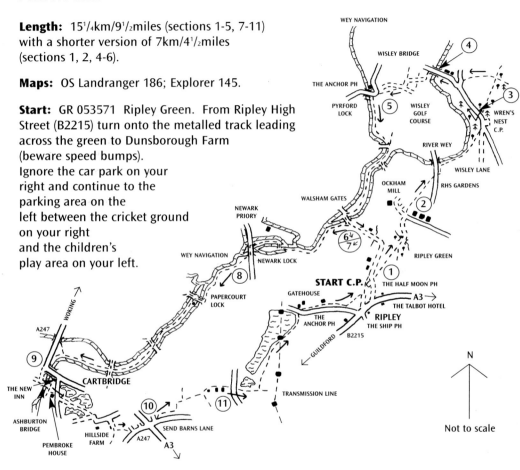

Transport: Buses from Woking, Guildford and Kingston pass through Ripley.

Refreshments: the Half Moon PH, the Ship PH, the Anchor PH, the Talbot Hotel and Watson's Bakery Tea Room, all in Ripley; the Anchor PH, Pyrford Lock; the New Inn, Cartbridge.

Introduction: This walk is flat and easy with only four stiles, though some sections can be muddy. A large section is on the towpath of the Wey Navigation which meanders through lovely meadows. The three locks with their passing boats are an added interest.

THE WALK

1. With your back to the children's play area, cross the entry track diagonally left and pass through a barrier at the corner of the cricket field by a 'No Horse Riding' sign. Take the left path going diagonally left across the open area of the green (not the path to the right of the hedge beside the cricket green). Half way across the green, look for a fingerpost (Public Footpath) on your right at the edge of the woods. Follow the direction of the fingerpost to bear left onto a path into the woods and at a T-junction, bear left along a bridleway to a footbridge. Cross the footbridge and continue along a muddy track to a road.

2. The walk continues straight on across the road to the fenced footpath opposite (a fingerpost indicates direction) but I strongly recommend a short detour to the left to see Ockham Mill (1862), now a private house, and the mill race and surrounding gardens. Retrace your steps back to **(2)** and continue on your route along the footpath which passes beside the grounds of the Royal Horticultural Gardens (RHS) at Wisley. You will see large white glasshouses over the fence on your right. Continue ahead to a private road; cross this and carry on along the path opposite, passing through a deer gate. The path bears right and for a short while runs alongside the River Wey on your left. It then continues between fences across the RHS gardens where you go over a small wooden bridge, through two metal gates and under a wooden bridge before passing through a second deer gate, where you emerge onto a concrete road. Turn left here and walk up to the tarmac road (Wisley Lane) and bear left along the pavement for approximately 100m/110yards. **To shorten the routes**, *continue along the road as far as Wisley Bridge and pick up the directions at section 4.*

3. Just past the Wren's Nest car park on your right there is a fingerpost (Public Footpath) on the same side of the road. Cross the road and follow the footpath into the woods. Continue through a gate in a fence and walk straight on until you come to a footpath junction with a waymark post (Permissive Horse Ride straight on or right). Here you bear left, eventually passing under a barrier (note the ditch on left). Continue to the next junction of paths and at a waymark post, turn left keeping the fence on your left and pass though a kissing gate. You will hear the roar of traffic and catch a brief glimpse of the M25 in the distance. Carry on ahead along a grassy track across a field to reach a stile. Go over the stile and turn left onto a concrete drive and continue to the road. Cross the road and turn right to walk along the pavement to reach Wisley Bridge.

4. Go over Wisley Bridge (River Wey) and immediately turn left over a stile (fingerpost - Public Footpath), to walk close to the river, then over a footbridge and onto a golf course (Wisley Golf Club). Turn right along the well laid sandy track, bearing left (ignore the path off right) and follow the track round to the left. At a Y-junction, look for a low white on blue sign (Public Footpath) by gorse bushes on your right - it may well be

concealed in long grass - and take the right fork onto another track. Continue on this track which emerges onto a road close to the Anchor public house which offers a refreshment stop where you can also watch boats going though Pyrford Lock.

5. Turning left, walk beside the lock, and follow the towpath on the Wey Navigation to Walsham Gates. This is the last remaining turf sided lock on the canal and was opened in 1653. It is not technically a lock as the gates are only closed in flood conditions. Cross the weir by the footbridge.

6. **For the shorter walk**, continue straight ahead from the weir, cross two footbridges followed by a brick-sided bridge, bearing right where the track becomes a private road, and follow this road back to your starting point.

7. **For the longer walk**, having crossed the weir, turn right onto the towpath and follow this path until you reach Newark Lock. Cross the bridge here and continue along the towpath again, noting the ruins of Newark Priory on your right. Unfortunately, these very evocative ruins are on private land and not open to the public. Continue on the towpath to Newark New Bridge (B367).

8. Turn left and cross the bridge with great care (one way traffic controlled by lights), and immediately turn right to continue on the towpath. At Papercourt Lock, cross over the footbridge, noting the inclined spill. Continue on the towpath for some 2km/1¼miles past the old tannery (now offices etc) to Cartbridge, passing the National Trust (NT) Cartbridge Wharf depot shortly before you reach the bridge. Go under the road bridge, then immediately turn sharp right up the steps to the road (A247).

9. Turn right over the road bridge and then right again to rejoin the towpath. The New Inn is on your left, and offers another refreshment stop. Continue on the towpath for a short distance passing Ashburton Bridge (a footbridge) on your right. Immediately after the last house on your left, turn left up a footpath by a green NT sign. Follow this narrow footpath to the road, cross over and turn right along the pavement for about 100m/110yards. At a fingerpost opposite Pembroke House, turn left along a broad tarmac track. Follow this track between two metal gates which lead to parking areas belonging to the Woking and District Angling Association, where it becomes a narrow fenced path passing between two fishing lakes. The path then bears right to a tarmac road (note Hillside Farm on your right). Turn left along the road and as soon as you see a sports field on your left, turn right into Farm Lane. This soon becomes a narrow track which starts to go slightly uphill. Look for a metal barrier on your left and turn left through this barrier, continuing along a narrow fenced path to a road (Send Hill). Turn left down the road to the traffic lights.

10. Cross over to Send Marsh Road (no sign) and continue past Maysfield Road on your left. Shortly afterwards, turn left at the fingerpost (Public Footpath) keeping to the left of a large wooden building ahead. Immediately after this building, turn right (note that the fingerpost at this junction does not have a 'finger' pointing to the right but your path, as indicated by the yellow arrow, is a right of way). Continue ahead following the line of a small stream on your left, cross a small footbridge over the stream and, follow the

path round to the right. Cross a larger footbridge, follow the path round to the left, and then shortly turn right at a post with a yellow waymark sign and follow the hedge round to the right. At a T-junction with a fingerpost turn left and follow the path round to the right and up to an old corrugated iron shed, crossing a small footbridge just before you reach it. Turn left to keep the shed on your right and continue along a grassy footpath between houses to your right and allotments on your left to a stile just before you reach the road (Polesden Lane).

11. Go over the stile and turn right along the road past Danesfield. Cross the road and go over another stile (fingerpost – Public Footpath). Continue ahead on the path to the left of the fence for about 300m/330yards; you may catch glimpses of the lake to your left behind the trees. At a Y-junction of paths, when electricity transmission lines and pylons come clearly into sight, bear diagonally left down a slight slope into trees. Follow this path through light woodland for about 600m/^{1}/$_3$mile until it comes out by a lake. (Note: there are various paths off to the left leading down to the lake but in wet weather great care should be taken as these turnings can be very soft underfoot.) Continue to follow the main path close to the water, passing close to a pylon, and then go round to the left at the end of the lake, where you will come to some open ground with a bench on your left and another pylon ahead. Turn right here to reach the road (Newark Lane), cross the road with care and turn right along the pavement. Immediately after the very ornate gatehouse and archway leading into Dunsborough Park, bear left onto Ripley Green, keeping beside the hedge on your left to reach the children's playground and return to your start point. There are both pubs and a tea shop in the village for refreshments at the end of your walk.

2 A 'stilish' walk - Normandy, Merrist Wood and Wood Street

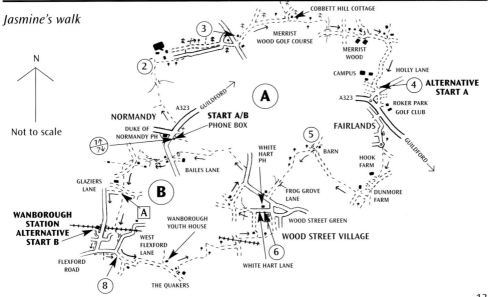

Jasmine's walk

N

Not to scale

Length: 11km/7miles - Circuit A (sections 1-6) or 7km/4¹/₂miles - Circuit B, a shorter loop via Flexford (sections 7, 8 and 6).

Maps: OS Landranger 186; Explorer 145.

Start: Circuits A and B: GR 927515   phone box beside the lay-by off Bailes Lane, Normandy at the junction with the A323 Guildford/Aldershot Road.

Alternative start for Circuit A: GR 964528   the entrance to Merrist Wood campus of Guildford College in Holly Lane off the A323. Parking is possible in the cul-de-sac leading to Roker Park Golf Club and Rokers Farm shop opposite the entrance to Merrist Wood. Start at section 4. This circuit could start with light refreshments at Roker Park Golf Club, continue to a visit to the White Hart, then stopping to watch the cricket, to walk on to the Duke of Normandy and return to Roker Park after stopping for a bar of chocolate and a soft drink at Merrist Wood, well refreshed and exercised!

Alternative start for Circuit B: GR 931503 Wanborough Station. Go left out of the station, walk up to the road and turn right onto Glaziers Lane. Follow this to the sharp bend and turn left along Flexford Road. Join the route at section 8 by walking ahead up West Flexford Lane, keeping Stream House on your right.

Transport: Buses between Guildford and Aldershot serve both starting points on or near the A323. Wanborough station is on the Gatwick/Guildford/Reading line.

Refreshments: the Duke of Normandy PH, Normandy; the White Hart PH, Wood Street; Roker Park Golf Club is open for light refreshments.

Introduction: This is an undulating walk with no hills but some good views; it can be muddy. Most of the walk is well signposted and parts are well trodden so should, I hope, be easy to follow. There are some 29 stiles along these two routes (counting them may keep children amused!) of which a number are now 'redundant' but have not been removed. Most of the walk is on uncultivated common land and in woods so there is an abundance of wildlife and mixed flora. There are bluebell woods, a spectacular snowdrop drift and ancient parkland trees. I have always met at least one deer, fox or rabbit on this walk. There is plenty of bird life; Broadstreet Common is excellent for jays, skylarks, magpies and green woodpeckers.

THE WALK

Circuit A (via Merrist Wood) 11km/7miles

1. From the phone box, walk back to the A323, turn right, go past the disused chapel and cross the main road with great care to the fingerpost opposite Chapel Farm Eggs. Follow the path in the direction of the fingerpost straight across this and the next field to a stile. This is a Countryside Commission Ecology Study Area - which means that wild

plants grow much as nature intended them to, and wildlife abounds including plenty of swifts screaming overhead in summer. At the stile, continue on the path as it goes almost straight ahead towards the right hand end of a large clump of trees where you will find a Victorian brick pedestrian bridge over a small stream. This is a nice place to sit and ponder who has used the bridge in years gone past, or enjoy a rest. Cross the bridge and follow the path ahead bearing slightly right till you reach a disused stile (waymarks for Fox Way and Footpath) beside a small metal gate. Go through the gate and continue ahead up the gentle slope, giving way to passing rabbits! At the end of the old walled garden on your right, turn right at the footpath T-junction.

2. Follow the footpath which runs along the bottom of the gardens of the rather imposing houses to the left and if you look to the right you may be able to see the Duke of Normandy pub. The last modern house has one of the largest cedar trees that you are likely to see. The path carries on between fences through light woodland where there is an abundance of snowdrops and bluebells in season. Continue straight on through the clearing till the fingerpost and waymarker indicate a left turn. Follow the path, cross a small tarmac road and turn right at the footpath T-junction. You now follow a long (500m/550yards) straight path that passes some magnificent chestnut, beech, oak and silver birch trees as well as rhododendrons that must have been part of the Henley Park estate at one time. Continuing straight on, re-cross the small road and eventually negotiate a metal kissing gate to reach a main road (Cobbett Hill Road).

3. Cross the road with care and go down the gravelled drive opposite which has a fingerpost and a large sign declaring Mercury Lodge Private Property. Having almost immediately passed a house on your left, continue on down the drive with Merrist Wood Golf Course on your right till you reach Cobbett Hill Cottage where you turn right following the footpath and keeping a leylandeii hedge on your left. After the next stile, go through the bracken and then a gap in the fence after which the path more or less follows the line of the right hand fence with Merrist Wood Golf Course on the other side. Just after the second gate/stile the path turns right at the fingerpost and after yet another stile reaches a track. Turn left over the bridge and go straight on till you see a wood on the left. Leave the track here, go over the stile into the wood and continue along it until you emerge onto the lawn of Merrist Wood. Bear right across this, heading for the road between the house on your right and the modern flat roofed buildings to the left. The next building on the right (Woody's Restaurant) has a chocolate and drinks machine outside and a handy bench to sit on. Continue down the road and turn right (signposted 'Way Out') to take the good footpath all the way down this road till you reach Holly Lane.

NOTE: *The alternative start point is the entrance to Merrist Wood campus in Holly Lane near the junction with the A323. Parking is possible at the far end of the cul de sac opposite which leads to Rokers Farm Shop and Roker Park Golf Club.*

4. Go over Holly Lane following the pavement past Fairlands Farm and Rokers Farm Shop on your left till you reach the A323; cross this carefully and turn left. Continue along the service road keeping the main A323 to your left. Cross Fairlands Avenue onto Fairlands Road and walk on until you reach a small roundabout where you will find a Broadstreet Common noticeboard on your left. Take the permissive footpath to the left of the board and follow this cinder-path, crossing the gravel drive leading to Hunts Farm (no sign) on your right. Go over the grass and into trees until you emerge onto an open area where there is a rustic bench. This part of Broadstreet Common is a good place to see skylarks, jays, green woodpeckers and magpies. With the bench on your left, follow the line of the hedge on your right. At Hook Farm, bear right along the track. At the metal scaffold pole, ignore the path to your right and go straight on and then take the waymarked footpath to the right. Dunmore Farm, the oldest house in the parish, is on your right. Do not enter the wood ahead but bear right to find a small wooden bridge. Go over this and follow the path along the fence at the bottom of Dunmore Farm's garden. Continue straight past the derelict buildings on the right down an ancient lane, go over two stiles and eventually emerge onto a track. Follow this track, bearing slightly right, until you see a small ancient barn in a tarmac turning circle ahead of you.

5. Just before you reach the barn, turn left to go over a concealed wooden bridge with a waymarker into the wood. Be careful here as it is easy to miss this turning! Follow the path bearing left through this lightly wooded area, then alongside a field. At the old wooden cross-country fence on your right, bear left and almost immediately turn right into the wood to follow the footpath. This is a good place for bluebells and deer. Continue slightly uphill past a pond on your left and over a stile into a field. Walk diagonally right across the field to go under the transmission cables roughly mid-way between the two poles. Behind a large dead tree stump you will find a stile leading to a bridge with concrete posts. Go over this and the bridge and follow the footpath till it meets Frog Grove Lane, by an electricity substation. Cross the road, turn left along the pavement and then right at Wood Street Green, where there are benches if you wish to picnic. Very shortly turn right down White Hart Lane to reach the White Hart pub.

6. With the pub on your right, continue on down the tarmac lane, which later becomes a gravelled path. At the cricket ground on your left, turn right to go through the car park and walk ahead down the tarmac track past Russellplace Farm. When you reach Frog Grove Lane, cross the road and turn left to walk along the pavement until you reach house number 70 on your right. Re-cross the road, and enter a large field at the waymarked stile. Walk diagonally right uphill across the field under the transmission line, over the brow of the hill, and go across the field in the same direction towards the hedge line ahead of you. At the hedge, turn left and follow the line of the hedge uphill to the corner of the field where you turn left again to follow the right hand hedge.

Very shortly, turn right over a stile. Go straight on towards the redundant stile in the middle of the field (there is no fence or hedge to negotiate!) to the crest of the hill; there is a good view from here. Continue straight on to the next waymarked stile, go over another stile and follow the line of the left hand fence. Exit the field by the stile next to the wrought iron gates to Bailes Farm. Turn right down Bailes Lane to the phone box. The Duke of Normandy pub is just round the corner to the left, on the main road.

Circuit B (via Flexford) 7km/4¹/₂miles

7. Starting at the phone box, turn left to walk up Bailes Lane and take the second footpath on the right, opposite Bailes Farm, also signposted 'Kelton' and 'Meadowside'. Walk between houses, go over a stile, then head diagonally right across a field, over a small bridge in the field and another in the trees where there is another stile. Cross this and bear diagonally left across a second field and then go over three stiles in succession. Follow the path to the hedge, bear left and continue alongside the hedge. Go over a stile, turn left onto a track and then immediately right; there is a chain link fence to your left. Continue straight on, ignoring the path to your right. **(A)** Go through a gate, turn left and you will see a fishing lake with water lilies on the left, and a chimney in the distance. The footpath crosses the railway line after which you turn immediately left along the footpath. Go over a stream, turn right following the stream past Little Flexford and on up the lane. At the fingerpost at the junction with West Flexford Lane, turn left.

*If you start the walk from Wanborough station, you join the route here. To return to the station after your walk, at point **(A)** above, turn right and walk along the path to reach Glaziers Lane where you turn left. Continue forward along the road for some 400m/¹/₄mile, go over the bridge and almost immediately turn right into the station approach road.*

8. Follow this lane/track for 800m/¹/₂mile, from which there are good views of the Hog's Back. Ignore the fingerpost to Wanborough Youth House and continue to the next fingerpost just before a house named The Quakers. Turn left onto the footpath, then left again to walk along a narrow path behind the garden of a house. Now turn right to walk up beside the field boundary on your right. At the next fingerpost turn half left cutting the corner of the field to go over the brow of the hill to the next fingerpost. Enter the wood and turn immediately left at the post. The footpath runs near the edge of this oak wood and eventually after 500m/550yards goes under the railway (good shelter in bad weather). Go over a stile, turn right and then immediately left at the post and rail barrier - do not go down the well-made path. Continue through the trees on this rougher track to the waymarker at the next rail and post barrier, and turn left. Go straight on, now walking on tarmac, till you reach Wood Street Green, turn left down White Hart Lane. The White Hart pub is on the right. **Now complete the walk by following the directions in section 6.**

3 Along the Pilgrims' Way to Albury and Chilworth

Anna's walk

Length: 13$\frac{1}{2}$km/8$\frac{1}{2}$miles with a shorter version of 6$\frac{1}{2}$km/4miles (sections 1-5 and 11).

Maps: OS Landranger 186; Explorer 145.

Start: GR 003484 Chantry Wood car park, Pilgrims Way, Guildford. Pilgrims Way is off the A281 between Guildford and Shalford opposite the southern end of Shalford Park. The entrance to the car park is to the right of a grassy triangle ahead as Pilgrims Way bears left.

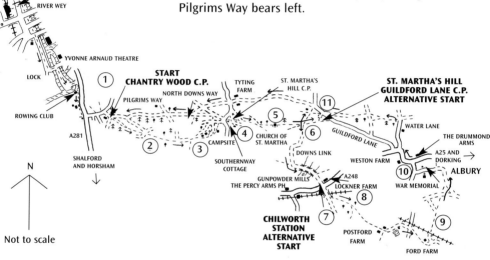

Not to scale

Alternative starts: GR 992496 Guildford railway station (see final section for instructions to the start at section 1); **or** GR 031472 Chilworth railway station (start at section 7); **or** GR 035485 St Martha's Hill Guildford Lane car park (start at section 11).

Transport: A number of bus routes to and from Guildford go along the A281. Chilworth railway station on the Reading/Guildford/Gatwick line is very close to the walk (start at section 7). Guildford railway station (London Waterloo/Portsmouth line) is 2km/1$\frac{1}{4}$miles away.

Refreshments: the Drummond Arms PH, Albury, on the route; the Percy Arms PH, Chilworth on the A248 near the route; wide selection of cafés, pubs and restaurants in Guildford.

18

Introduction: This is a walk with many lovely views and opportunities to spot Surrey village church towers on the way and to visit St Martha's church, the oldest part of which dates from 1190. This church, which can only be reached on foot, stands 175metres/577feet above sea level and is situated near the Pilgrims' Way from Winchester to Canterbury. Following the murder in 1170 of Thomas à Becket, pilgrims called at St Martha's on their way to Canterbury. It is said to be the only church in Britain dedicated to St Martha.

THE WALK

1. With your back to the vehicular entrance to the Chantry Wood car park, take the pedestrian exit in the far right hand corner, go diagonally right towards the Guildford Borough sign for Chantry Wood (ignoring all other paths and tracks) and turn left into the reserve. Turn immediately right and take the footpath off right which passes a notice board and a wooden shed on your right, ignoring the path to your left (Scholars' Trail) and the broad track straight ahead with seats on either side. Climb the broad shallow steps and follow the sandy path uphill through the wood, noting the wooden bench on the left and later the large seat on your right where you get good views of Shalford. Carry on uphill ignoring all other tracks. Very shortly before the top of the hill, the main path bears left at a wooden waymark post with butterfly, bird and deer head carvings. Continue on the minor path to the right of the waymark going downhill through the trees, passing a wooden handrail/barrier on the right and descend steps, to go over a stile. Go along the path ahead towards a wood with an open view of fields and Shalford to your right (but ignore the path downhill in this direction).

2. At the top of the hill, ignore the small path to your right and continue straight on through an open field. Continue to the far side with a wood on your left and views to your right. A path (Scholars' Trail) joins from your left just by a wooden bench dedicated to Robin and Una Graham. Shortly, pass the gated main path from your left and go straight along the track passing a hedge with a waymark post on your right which indicates a footpath going off downhill. Ahead of you on the wooded hill you can see the tower of the church of St Martha.

3. Go along the track across a field, passing a Scholars' Trail waymark on your left and continue along the track with open views to your right. Go forward out into open space and on across it, to pass through a narrow belt of trees and bear right keeping the main woodland to your left. Cross an open field with a large wooden hut and other buildings on your left. At the end of the field, note the water tank on your right and bear left in front of it to enter a wood (sign Private Campsite). Continue along the overgrown main vehicular track, first forking right and then bearing right until you pass a metal vehicle barrier by another 'Private Campsite' sign and join a road.

4. At a fingerpost (North Downs Way) turn left onto the road, and after 30m/33yards turn right onto the North Downs Way (NDW) uphill with Southernway cottage immediately on your right and later houses called Southernway and St Martha's Priory also on your right.

Continue past the vehicle barrier along a wide sandy track. At a fork with a bridleway to the right, continue straight along the footpath; there is a waymark on your right with a plaque of the outline of the church. To the right are views of Chilworth. Enter St Martha's churchyard from the west, pass in front of the church, and enjoy the views from here as you can see as far as the South Downs and Black Down on a clear day.

5. Leave the churchyard by the east gate with Yvonne Arnaud's grave immediately on your right. Continue straight on the sandy path downhill with a wooden barrier on your right. At a fingerpost, where a bridleway joins on your right, continue straight on 50m/55yards ahead to the Downs Link notice board. **To shorten your walk,** *turn left here and walk along the NDW until you reach the road. You will pass the St Martha's Hill Guildford Lane car park off to your right. Pick up the walk at section 11 below.*

6. Turn sharp right along the Downs Link footpath, and follow the path downhill with views on your left of Albury church and fields on either side. The path turns sharp right and later left to reach a T-junction of paths. Turn left, still following the Downs Link path and after passing a very overgrown World War II concrete tank barrier on your right, cross three bridges over the Tilling Bourne and old canal. (Immediately after the concrete bridge, a path goes off right, beside the stream where a notice board on 'A Damnable Invention' gives information about the Chilworth gunpowder industry.) Continue straight along the track ignoring the footpath on your left. Pass Lockner Farm livery stables to reach a road (A248); cross this carefully.

If you start the walk from Chilworth station, *turn right outside the station and walk along the main road for about 450m/500yards until you reach a bus stop and the Downs Link bridleway where you turn right.*

7. Follow the Downs Link bridleway ahead going slightly uphill. Cross the railway bridge and, with Lockner Lodge on your left, turn immediately left onto a waymarked footpath to go across a field, over a stile and head diagonally right towards trees. If you look back, there is an excellent view of St Martha's church on the hill.

8. Cross two stiles to go through trees into the Albury Estate. Follow the direction of the fingerpost to take the path to your right across a field and come out of the estate with a Victorian cottage on your right. Follow the metalled track downhill (ignore the footpath on your right) past a farm building on your left. After passing a large pond on your right and going slightly uphill continue forward ignoring the stile leading to a footpath on your left. At the end of Postford Farm track, turn right at a fingerpost 20m/22yards downhill and then go left over a stile. Follow the footpath with a stream and a trout farm on your right, and continue straight ahead at the telegraph pole. Do look back to spot St Martha's again. Leave the field via a kissing gate and turn left into the farm buildings of Ford Farm, and left again immediately onto a bridleway with a metal gate, passing an old cottage on your left. Continue through the metal gate uphill through a tunnel of trees and cross the railway line with care.

9. Continue straight ahead uphill across the field towards woods ahead. Go over a stile on your right into a wood and carry straight on, ignoring all side tracks, until you cross a bridleway. Then walk downhill on an enclosed path, keeping the fence on your left, till you reach a T-junction and then turn left onto a bridleway and continue downhill to Albury (ignore the stile on your right). You will reach a metalled road with cottages on either side; ignore the footpath off to your right and walk on past Albury Church and then the war memorial on your right. Continue to the T-junction and turn right onto the road to go downhill through the village. Cross the road (A248) carefully. *If you need a refreshment stop, turn right at the main road for the Drummond Arms, and when you leave the pub turn right and stay on the same side of the road to pick up the route below.*

10. Turn left to go past the post office and village store on your right, and then cross the road back again to pick up the pavement on the other side to pass Weston Farm on your left. After 300m/330yards, turn right and go over the road (take great care as this is a blind bend) into Water Lane, and follow the road (no pavements) uphill passing converted farm buildings on your right. Continue uphill until you reach a bridleway sign on your left. Turn sharply left onto the bridleway and follow the path uphill through a lightly wooded area with a view to your right of Albury Downs and Newlands Corner. When you reach an open field, cross diagonally right following the clear track to the hedge ahead with a farm on your right. Leave the field through a gate, and continue straight on uphill, ignoring footpaths to your left and right. This path, which has a field on the right and a wood on the left, goes uphill beside the wood to start with and then levels out with fields on both sides. Continue until you reach a road where you turn right to walk along it for 300m/330yards going gently downhill and passing St Martha's Hill Guildford Lane car park on your left. There are views of the Downs on your right.

11. **Resume the short walk here.** At a bend in the road marked White Lane/Guildford Lane, turn left onto a bridleway by a wooden gate (ignore the NDW to the left and right). Go straight ahead passing a second gate and dilapidated buildings on your left and continue on for some distance eventually passing through a disused farm (Tyting Farm). At the farm gate by Tyting Lodge, cross the road onto a bridleway and go straight on. At the crossing of paths by the Pewley Downs notice board on your right, continue straight ahead into the wood. Here the main path bears left, then right (joined on the left by a bridleway with an acorn waymark indicating the NDW). Do not take the path ahead uphill but instead bear right along a track with open fields on both sides. Continue through a wooded area and at crossing paths (with livery stables off to your right) continue straight on the main track on Pilgrims Way, go across the fields and with the first Guildford houses up on your right, continue straight on a short distance to reach the Chantry Wood car park.

If starting the walk at Guildford railway station, leave by the main entrance and cross the small car park ahead following the signs for North Guildford and the cinema. Cross Walnut Tree Close, turn left and then immediately right to go down steps beside the entrance to a pedestrian bridge over the river Wey. Turn right and walk along the tow path passing under three bridges. Continue straight ahead across the end of the fourth (Town Bridge) to pick up the tow path again. Continue forward walking through a car park beside the river and then turn left to cross the river over a black and white painted iron bridge. Turn right to walk beside the lock and follow the path ahead bearing left to a concrete bridge. Cross the river here and before reaching the road, go down the steps on your right to walk across the entrance to the Guildford Rowing Club. Follow the tarmac track ahead, alongside the A281 on your left and the water meadows on your right. (If these are flooded, cross the road to use the pavement.) Continue past playing fields and a sports pavilion on your right, to reach Pilgrims Way, the second turning on the left, opposite a fingerpost (Bridleway) indicating the route of the NDW. Turn left to walk up Pilgrims Way, pass two turnings to the right and reach the Chantry Wood car park behind the grassy triangle off right. Follow the instructions from section 1.

Note. Walks 3 and 4 both explore the areas around St Martha's and Chilworth. They overlap between sections 3: 6, 7, 8, and 4: 1, 2. See sketch maps.

4 An introduction to the Surrey Hills - Tilling Bourne Valley, Albury Heath and Shere

Peter H's walk

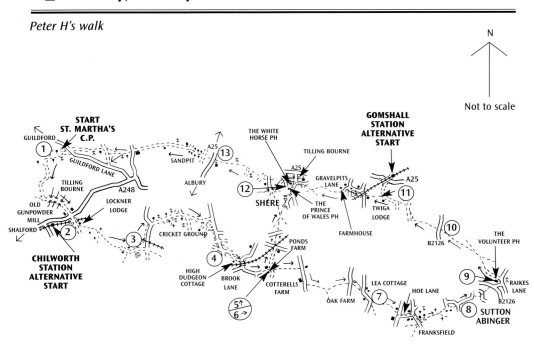

Length: 18km/11¼miles (sections 1-4, 6-13) with a shorter version of 12km/7½miles (sections 1-5, 12 and 13).

Maps: OS Landranger 186 and 187; Explorer 145 and 146.

Start: GR 035485 St Martha's Hill Guildford Lane car park.
Guildford Lane can be reached from the A248 Shalford/Albury road to the south; from Epsom Road (A246) at Guildford, turn into Warren Road, go right into One Tree Hill and then left into White Lane which leads to Guildford Lane.

Alternative Starts: GR 031472 Chilworth station, 400m/¼mile from the route (start at section 2);
or GR 089478 Gomshall station 200m/220yards from the route (start at section 11).

Transport: Both Chilworth and Gomshall stations are on the Reading/Guildford/Gatwick line. Buses from Guildford to Dorking, Reigate, Redhill and Cranleigh go along the A248/A25, passing Chilworth and Gomshall stations.

Refreshments: the Volunteer PH, Sutton Abinger; the Prince of Wales PH, the White Horse PH, the Lucky Duck Tea Room, all in Shere village.

Introduction: This route includes some lovely parts of the Surrey Hills, an Area of Outstanding Natural Beauty (AONB). It has good views of the Tilling Bourne valley and the North Downs, passes the old Chilworth gunpowder mill and a D-Day memorial stone and returns through the picturesque village of Shere.
While the route avoids any steep climbs it may be muddy in places during wet periods, although it is virtually mud free during drier summer periods as it crosses heathland for a good part of the way.

THE WALK

1. From the car park with your back to the road, take the path immediately to the left of the notice board. Bear right as a path merges from the left, following signs for the 'self guided trail'. Turn right on reaching a main sandy path. Follow the path as it starts to ascend, looking out on your left hand side for the notice board marking the start of the Downs Link path. Turn left onto this path and follow it down. On reaching a T-junction with a gate opposite, turn left to continue following the Downs Link. At the bottom of the slope carry on along the track as it goes around to the right, crossing the Tilling Bourne. Continue up the track and, immediately before the old canal, look out on your right for a path and a notice about the Old Gunpowder Mill. A slight diversion along this path will take you to the remains of the buildings. Re-trace your steps back past the notice board and turn right back onto the main (Downs Link) track. Continue over the old canal and follow the track straight ahead, passing the Lockner Farm Livery Stables, to reach the main road (A248). Go directly across and up the lane on the opposite side.

If starting from Chilworth station, *leave the station to come out onto the main road, turn right and staying on the same side of the road, walk along until you reach a bus stop/shelter, opposite Lockner Farm Livery Stables. Turn right onto the Downs Link to go up the lane.*

2. Cross over the railway bridge and immediately past Lockner Lodge take the footpath on the left. Follow the path diagonally left across this field, cross the stile and take the path across the next field, bearing slightly to the right. Cross two stiles through a short wooded section and, turning right, continue along the path in the next field following the line of trees on your right hand side. Continue straight ahead across this field aiming to the right of a row of trees. Follow the track with these trees on your left. Continue past cottages on your right and farm buildings, following the track down and around to the left, cross the small stream, pass a pond on your right and go uphill. Immediately after a 90° bend to the right around a farm building look out for a stile on your left hand side. Cross the stile and follow the path diagonally to your right across the field to reach the railway.

3. Take care as you cross the railway track and follow the path directly ahead on the other side. On emerging into a road, go straight across and follow the path uphill on the other side. At the top, continue following this sandy track straight ahead, ignoring all paths to the right and left. Emerging into an open area past a small wooden fence on your right hand side, take the fork to your right. Follow this sandy track directly ahead, crossing a track to the cottages on your right. As you descend the gentle slope, take the sandy track on the left hand side of the fork, continuing ahead across another drive and up the slope. On reaching the tarmac drive, turn to your right to the small car park and then go immediately to the left and follow the track, with the trees to your left and Albury cricket ground on your right hand side. As you get towards the end of the cricket ground, look out on your left for a memorial stone marking the point where Field Marshall Sir Bernard Montgomery (Monty) addressed the Canadian troops in May 1944 prior to the D-Day landings. Continuing straight ahead beyond the cricket pitch, go between the wooden posts, walk beyond the small parking area, and take the left hand fork, to remain parallel with the road on your left. As you emerge onto a main cross path, bear left and out onto a road.

4. Go directly across the road, with care, and take the track on the other side. At the fork, take the right hand track, and go past a cross track and a brick building on your left hand side. As you pass High Dudgeon Cottage on your right hand side, look for a path (waymarker on your left hand side) that leads directly off a small concrete ramp. Follow this path gently downhill to a road, Brook Lane. Turn right to walk carefully (no pavements) under a railway bridge and immediately turn left to take the drive to Ponds Farm.

Keep following the drive with the field on your left hand side and ignore the path that turns off to the right. On reaching the buildings at the farm take the stile immediately to the left hand side of the gate into Ponds House. As you emerge onto a cross path, **this is the point where you can take the shorter 12km/7¹/₂mile route.**

Shorter Walk

5. Turn left onto the cross path, a green lane, and follow it until you emerge into an open area with some cottages on your right. Then look out for the gate on your left, and take care as you cross the railway tracks; once across take the first path on the right into lightly wooded heathland. Ignore an unmarked cross path and continue ahead on the left hand fork as paths cross. On reaching a road, cross carefully and take the bridleway directly opposite; continue ahead when a path forks off to the left. After a short descent, continue ahead as a path forks in from the left and then as another path forks in from the right. After a short distance, take the bridleway ahead that turns off to the right towards open fields. Go up a short slope and then descend, and as you reach the houses, take the road directly ahead. As this road turns to the right, before it descends to the main road, take the path that forks off on the left, go directly over the drive and continue on the path opposite. At the next drive, continue directly ahead, slightly to your left. When you reach the low wall directly ahead of you, follow the drive around to the right, taking you out to the road. Take care as you turn left onto the road, moving across to the right hand side to walk on the pavement. Continue down the road and you rejoin the longer walk in front of the White Horse, just before reaching the Tilling Bourne stream. **Now follow the directions in sections 12 and 13.**

Longer Walk

6. Continue on the longer walk by going up the path on the opposite bank, marked as the 'Shere Parish Millennium Trail' (SPMT). Go through the gate at the top and go directly ahead across the field aiming slightly to the left of the building in the distance. As you emerge onto the road, be careful now as there is a small section of road walking. Turn right along the road, pass the entrance to Cotterells Farm and as you reach the end of the barn on your right, cross the road and take the path on the left (fingerpost - Public Bridleway), following the SPMT. Continue along this path, ignoring the stile into the field on the right hand side, and go directly across another small road to go through a gate, remaining on the SPMT. Follow this grass track as it continues directly ahead and bears around to the right. Eventually the track turns to the left for you to emerge through a gate and onto a small road opposite Lea Cottage. Turn right to follow this quiet road. After passing Oak Farm and as the road bears around to the right, look out for a footpath on your left hand side. Be careful here, as there are two footpaths leaving the road on the left hand side very close to each other.

7. You should take the first of these two paths, and go over the stile by the first field gate. At this point you are leaving the SPMT. Follow the path as it veers slightly to the right and then twists back to the left, through the field towards the hedge ahead.

Cross the stile and continue directly ahead in the next field. Keeping the hedge on your left hand side, pass a gap and continue with the hedge remaining on your left. Cross the stile out of the field and continue ahead, eventually turning left out onto a road (Pursers Lane). Turn right for a short distance on the footpath by the side of the road and almost immediately take Hoe Lane on your left. Continue up the road past Hoe Farm on your right and at the T-junction turn right into Franksfield, a no through road. After passing Keepers Cottage on the left, take the footpath down the following track on your left, which again takes you onto the SPMT. Follow this private drive to Timbers Ridge. Pass Timbers Ridge on your left hand side. Cross the stile and continue straight ahead across the field. Cross another stile and follow the path downhill directly ahead. At the bottom, continue directly ahead, ignoring the path on your right. Go up the slope, then steps and over the stile. As you emerge onto a drive, continue along the footpath directly in front of you. Alma Cottage is on your right.

8. Emerging onto another drive, turn to the left and take the right hand fork at the almost immediate junction. As the road descends and bears to the left, take the public footpath on the right hand side, go over a stile and up a short ascent. Go ahead with a field on your right until you reach the next drive where you turn left. Walk a very short distance before taking the path on your right hand side that goes between two fields. As you reach the brow of the hill you can see the Volunteer pub directly ahead of you. Continue along the fenced path going downhill and take care as you emerge onto this busier road. Turn right to follow it for a short distance before turning left into Raikes Lane, which takes you to the Volunteer pub.

9. The walk continues up Raikes Lane with the Volunteer pub on your left hand side. After a short distance, take the public bridleway which turns uphill on your left hand side. Follow this track to reach the gateway into The Sheiling, a private entrance. At this point take the narrow bridleway on the right hand side of the entrance. As you emerge into the field, continue ahead with the tree line on your right and fencing on your left hand side. At the junction of paths, turn left on a bridleway to follow the line of the fencing. As the path turns to the right, there is a hedge and row of trees between you and the field on your left. On reaching an opening through the hedge and trees, turn left through the opening and follow the footpath on the other side of the hedge, now on your right. Cross the stile and continue ahead on the path across the next field, following the line of the overhead cables. Exit this field over a stile and continue downhill passing Oxmoor Copse, a small Woodland Trust property, on your left. Go over the stile out onto a road (B2126).

10. Cross carefully and take the path directly opposite. Ignore the field entrance on your left and follow the path, which may be a bit overgrown in places, eventually emerging over a stile into a field. Continue straight across this field, heading to the left hand side of a row of trees. Carry on ahead beyond the trees until you reach the boundary of the field and, staying within the field, turn right. Follow along the edge of this field and the path will eventually turn left through the tree line and go down, via a stile, onto a lower path. Turn right on this lower bridleway and then keep looking out on your left

hand side for a path into a field. Turn left onto this path to go diagonally right downhill across the field. After crossing the field, continue ahead on a track merging from the right. Turn to the right at the next junction. As this main track turns 90° to the right, with a 'Private, No Public Right of Way' gateway that is immediately in front of you and Twiga Lodge on your left, follow the main track around to the right, and then immediately take the public bridleway off to your left.

If joining the walk from Gomshall station, from the car park turn left downhill on the station approach road and at the bottom, cross Station Road (A25) with great care. Turn left to walk under the railway and then right into Wonham Way a wide gravel track (fingerpost - Public Footpath). Continue over the stream, pass a house on your left and with Twiga Lodge ahead of you, turn right immediately after a wooden gate to take the public bridleway on your right.

11. Continuing along this path which merges with a track on your left hand side, follow it as it bears around slightly to the right. As you emerge on to a road, turn right and walk underneath the railway. At the road junction, turn left and follow this road, High View. As you pass the bus stop and post box on your right hand side, take the right fork at the triangle down to the road junction. Go directly across the road into Gravelpits Lane. Take the first left hand fork and immediately in front of Gravelpits Farmhouse, take the bridleway to your right. Once again you are on the SPMT. Continue along this path ignoring any path off and as you approach Shere village the church will come into view on your right hand side. Upon reaching crossing paths, take the right hand path that leads you to the church, again on the SPMT, to emerge into a road. Walk along the road with the church on your right. Cross the road at the junction in front of the White Horse pub and go right, and almost immediately, turn left along Lower Street.

12. Continue the shorter walk here. With the Tilling Bourne stream on your right, pass the Old Jail House on your left. Where the road turns to the right across the ford, go straight ahead, towards the Old Rectory. Continue straight ahead past the bridge on your right to the Old Rectory. Go through a kissing gate, again marked with the SPMT, and continue with the stream still on your right. As you emerge through Vicky's Gate turn right over the footbridge by the ford over the stream. Continue up the lane past Chantry Lane Cottage on your left, then look out for a path crossing the lane. On reaching the path turn left up the slope. Go through a metal kissing gate keeping to the left hand side of the field. Go through the next metal kissing gate into a wooded area and continue straight ahead. As you emerge from the wooded area, cross a stile into a field and continue ahead with a fence on your left hand side. As the field opens up bear slightly right towards the trees ahead. Cross the stile and go down the track to the road (A248).

13. Take care as you cross this road and go over the stile directly opposite. Cross a stream and a second stile, continuing straight ahead. Go over another stile out of this field and keep forward along the path passing the gates to the former sand pit on your left hand side.

As you merge with a track from your right, continue straight ahead. Cross another stile and walk past a cottage on your left hand side. At the junction continue ahead to the left downhill passing by a metal gate and then cottages on your left to reach a small road. Turn left and almost immediately ascend the path on the right hand side. Continue along this path through light woodland and through a gateway. Follow the path as it bears around to the left and then goes diagonally slightly right across a field. Emerging from the field through a gate, go over a crossing footpath and continue directly ahead. On reaching the road take the bridleway, slightly offset to the right, opposite, which will soon bring you back to the starting car park.

Note. Walks 3 and 4 both explore the areas around St Martha's and Chilworth. They overlap between sections 3: 6, 7, 8 and 4: 1, 2. See sketch maps.

5 Dog walking at its best on Surrey woodland and commons - Ranmore and Effingham

Viv's walk with Barney

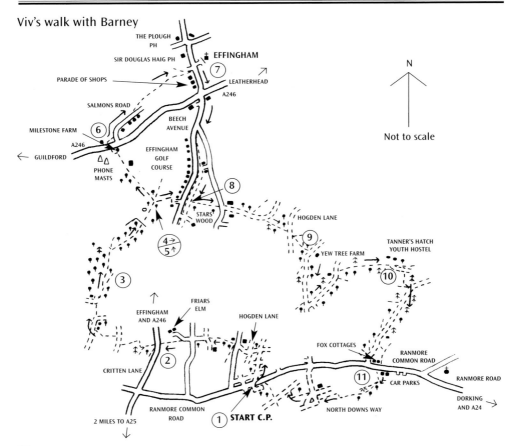

Length: 12$\frac{1}{2}$km/7$\frac{3}{4}$miles (sections 1-3, 5-11) with a shorter route of 10km/6$\frac{1}{4}$miles (sections 1-4, 8-11).

Maps: OS Landranger 187; Explorer 146.

Start: GR 127502 National Trust Ranmore Common car park, an enclosed car park on Ranmore Common Road, 5km/3miles west of Dorking.
From Dorking (A24) take the A2003 and at a mini roundabout turn into Ranmore Road which continues into Ranmore Common Road.
From the A246 Guildford to Leatherhead road, at Effingham crossroads and traffic lights, turn into Beech Avenue, which later becomes Critten Lane, and continue for 3km/2miles to crossroads. Turn left along Ranmore Common Road; the car park is on your right in about 800m/$\frac{1}{2}$mile.
From the A25 Guildford to Dorking road, at a small crossroads 2km/1$\frac{1}{4}$miles west of Abinger Hammer, turn up a small lane signed to Effingham and at crossroads at the top turn right for about 800m/$\frac{1}{2}$mile to the car park on your right.

Transport: Buses from Guildford, Leatherhead, Epsom and Dorking pass along the A246 through Effingham (start the walk at section 7).

Refreshments: the Sir Douglas Haig PH, the Plough PH, Watsons Bakery, (refreshments) all in Effingham.

Introduction: Barney is my field spaniel and we enjoy doing this walk together in all seasons. Three stiles have dog gates, but four need the dog to be carried across, due to strong sheep fencing. Most dogs should be able to negotiate the remaining stiles by themselves but will need to be kept on the lead across the golf course.

The walk offers a gentle undulating route with mixed landscape and views over the Thames Valley and hidden valleys around Polesden Lacey (National Trust). You pass through Ranmore Common, along ancient green lanes, across stock fields, arable land, managed hazel and chestnut woodland and old woodland where you will find some magnificent great beech, oak and yew trees. Some bridleways are invariably muddy throughout the year. Woodland flowers, especially bluebells are abundant (April/May) and in high summer you have the benefit of shade.

THE WALK

1. From the car park, face the road and take the left hand exit (west end). Cross straight over, with great care, to an opening, a little to the right, by a blue arrowed marker post. Go ahead along a broad grassy bridleway. At the third crossing path (including the path very near the road), marked by a National Trust (NT) post with blue waymarks, turn left to go between large oak trees and follow the path as it heads downhill. Cross the wide

track (Hogden Lane) and go ahead around the boundary of a house on your right, joining the track that serves the house and follow that, crossing another road and continue onwards. The path narrows, goes downhill and becomes another driveway that goes between fenced fields and then up to a road. Cross the road into the drive of Friars Elm. At a curve in the drive, continue straight on, over a stile (three dog gates make this stretch much easier for canine friends). The path follows the edge of two fields, and continues downhill in a third to a gate onto a road. Caution here, as traffic often goes at speed on this section.

2. Cross the road and take a narrow path at the edge of the wood that keeps alongside the margin of the field to your right. After crossing two stiles, bear to the right (notice arrow on tree) and head to some trees to cross another stile just before them. This brings you into a large field. Turn left and follow the field edge to a gate/stile on the far side. Go through/over, turn right into a green lane and almost immediately go through a gate passing between field hedges, and then cross the first stile you reach on the left. Follow the right edge of the field to another stile into a wood. Follow the path downhill through the wood for a short way, and cross another stile onto a path to the left of a house. This path emerges onto a drive serving a few houses. Turn right past the houses and onwards along a bridleway that leads you into a wood after passing a fenced field on the right. At a junction in the path, with a small coach house facing you, bear right onto the lesser path (still a bridleway) further into the wood. This woodland is delightful the year round with abundant spring woodland plants under young beech and hazel coppicing, and pleasant dappled shade on hot summer days.

3. Continue along this path and at a fork, bear to the left, slightly uphill. When you reach a field, cross the stile and follow the left hand field edge to the left hand corner of the field to cross over another stile. Turn right and go through an old iron fence passing two grey metal gates through more woodland and follow this path until it emerges into the open at a golf course (Effingham). Here you have superb views north across the Thames Valley on a clear day. Do take care as you walk on the golf course! Keep forward across the fairway going slightly right of the sand bunker ahead of you and make for the clump of trees. Here look for a marker post with yellow arrow and follow the direction indicated into woodland, to reach a junction with a crossing path and another marker post. It is here that the walk divides.

Shorter walk (Note: this route has no refreshment stops)

4. Turn right on a small path through the wood and continue straight across a wide track, by another marker post, to reach the edge of the woodland where another marker post directs you straight forward across the fairway to the left of the hedge line opposite. Another marker post here directs you to bear right onto a path going into the bushes. The path goes beside a house onto a drive and emerges at the road. Cross this minor road carefully as cars speed up it, to go straight over onto a path which almost immediately bears left to reach a stile beside a metal gate on your right. Go over the stile. You are now at Stars Wood where the longer and shorter routes rejoin.
Rejoin the main walk at section 8.

Longer Walk

5. Turn left, with another marker post as you emerge from the woodland, and keep ahead following a series of marker posts. As you reach a disused tee on the far side of the golf course, you will see a fingerpost beyond it and two phone masts in the distance. From the fingerpost continue in the same direction diagonally across the corner of the field ahead. I have found this path well-marked at all times of year. The path heads towards and through a line of trees and then continues in the same direction across another field, and into a third field beyond a further line of trees. The path (now fainter) then crosses another fairway (beware of golfers and their balls!) through rough grass heading left for a stile in front of farm buildings. The phone masts are now on your left. Go over the stile, turn left and take the fenced path which skirts the buildings. Go through a wooden gate into another fenced path along the right hand edge of a field which then emerges via a gate onto the A246 beside Milestone Farm. Please take special care crossing this main road; it is very hazardous on this stretch due to the speed of traffic.

6. Cross over and turn right. There is a marked bridleway after the end house that follows the line of the road and brings you to Salmons Road. Turn left, follow Salmons Road until you reach a fingerpost (Public Bridleway) on your left. Follow this bridleway diagonally across the corner of the field to a gap in the hedge. Go through this and continue along the bridleway (which can be rather overgrown with stinging nettles in high summer) until you reach a driveway that emerges at a parade of shops (including a cafe/bakery) in Effingham village. Turn left for both pubs. The Sir Douglas Haig is on the same road and The Plough is further on and left at the mini-roundabout. St Lawrence Church and churchyard is well worth a visit (go up Crossways, opposite the shopping parade). There is also a pretty church garden opposite the church on Browns Lane. Another interesting sight in that road is a corner house with several trompe l'oeil features. After a rest and refreshment, the walk continues by returning to the parade of shops.

7. At the parade of shops cross the road and turn right to walk along the road through Effingham and then bear left on the track away from the road to cross the main road (A246) at traffic lights. Turn left to walk up Beech Avenue. Beware, the road is narrow and so is the pavement until past Effingham Golf Clubhouse on your right. A path continues on the right behind trees. Follow this path uphill until you have passed the golf course and reach some houses on your right. At the second driveway, leading to Ranmore and Wildways, turn left and cross the road going diagonally right to take the footpath (fingerpost) on the other side of the road by a pumping station. Follow this path that weaves uphill parallel to the road through a belt of trees for some way, ignoring the drive on the left to some houses where the path broadens. At the end of the fields on the left, turn left onto a path and then go over a stile on your left. At this point the shorter route rejoins the longer route.

8. **Continue the short walk here.** Follow the path across the top of the field, with Stars Wood on your right, heading east and cross the stile onto a road and into a driveway opposite. The bridleway (the signpost is hidden by overhanging trees) goes between two properties and leads into NT land; this path can be quite muddy most of the year as it is well shaded. Continue on the same bridleway as it passes a horse field. Ignoring a path to the left, bear right and downhill with another field to the left to emerge onto Hogden Lane, a bridleway. Turn right for a short distance and beside a bridleway on the left, go through a kissing gate into a steep field. The path crosses this field diagonally, uphill to another gate. Go through the gate and cross a bridleway into another field by a gate. From the far side of this field, you will have excellent views of Polesden Lacey, a Regency villa and its gardens owned by the National Trust.

9. Go through a gate at the top right of this field heading to the right past Yew Tree Farm on a wide track (south) with blue waymarks. There are several good viewpoints along this path (where you are kindly provided with benches to sit on) that climbs gradually uphill in mature beech woods. After passing two fields on the left with a strip of woodland between them, take a path to the left that is marked by a NT waymarker post, and continue until you reach a wide bridleway. At this junction there is a great beech tree to admire. Turn left and follow the bridleway on downhill to a cottage. By the house gate, turn right and follow the undulating course of the path until you reach Tanner's Hatch Youth Hostel, enjoying more good views of Polesden Lacey on the way.

10. Ignoring the first right turn at the Youth Hostel, go ahead to stand by the gate into the hostel. Immediately opposite the gate is a track. Take this track which forks immediately and take the right (uphill) path. At the next fork, bear right on a footpath that weaves under trees and becomes a muddy bridleway for a short section, with a large coppiced chestnut plantation on the left and larch and mature mixed woods on the right. At a junction, turn right onto a wide track and follow it until you reach Ranmore Common Road emerging at Fox Cottages.

11. Cross the road diagonally left to a fingerpost indicating a path south into woodland. Go down this path till it meets a wide track, signed North Downs Way (NDW). Turn left along it very briefly and enter Steers Field (NT), from where there are sweeping views over the valley between Dorking and Westcott and the hills beyond. Head right, downhill, following the wooded field edge on your right and at the bottom of the field go through a weighted gate onto downland. Turn right and follow the clear chalky path, staying parallel with the hillside and a fence. Follow the path uphill and go through the third kissing gate in the fence on your right, at the end of a field, onto the NDW. Turn left and then very shortly, at a fingerpost, turn right onto a public byway. Follow this to the Dorking Scout Campsite and turn left onto a grassy path through young woodland. Take the next right and continue, with young dense beech woods on the left; in April/May bluebells abound. At the end of this path, turn left onto a wide grassy path, always cool in summer, and continue ahead. At the next small crossing path, turn right, where you will have a tall Scots pine plantation on your left and birch on the right. Follow this grassy path to the end and turn left onto a rutted/muddy bridleway which leads across gorse scrub and grass back to the car park.

6 A woodland, farmland and river walk from Godalming towards Munstead and Eashing

Damian and Elizabeth's walk

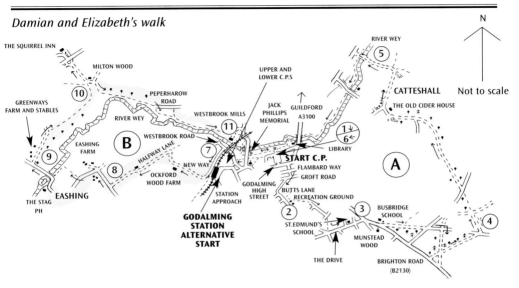

Length: A figure of eight walk centred on Godalming of 15km/9¼miles, with one walk towards Munstead of 8km/5miles, Circuit A on sketch map, (sections 1-5) and another towards Eashing of 7km/4¼miles, Circuit B on sketch map, (sections 6-11).

Maps: OS Landranger 186; Explorer 145.

Start: GR 972441 Crown Court car park, The Burys, Godalming (see sketch map).

Alternative start: GR 966439 Godalming station is about 600m/⅓mile from the car park (see directions below).

Transport: Several bus routes to/from Guildford and Haslemere serve the centre of Godalming. Godalming station is on the London Waterloo/Portsmouth line.

Refreshments: Wide selection of cafés, restaurants and public houses in Godalming; Hector's on the Wey café (Circuit A); the Stag PH, Eashing; the Squirrel Inn, Hurtmore (Circuit B) can easily be reached (see sketch map).

Introduction: We like this walk as it gives us a chance to see a wide variety of places in and around our local town - the Lammas Lands in the centre of Godalming, the Parish Church, the Town Bridge, the River Wey, the Old Bridge at Eashing and views from Munstead Heath. We're looking forward to taking our grandchildren on this route when they are older.

THE WALK

Circuit A (via Munstead/Catteshall) 8km/5miles

To reach the start of this section of the walk from Godalming railway station, come out of the main entrance and bear left down Station Approach and keep left on a short section of footpath, passing to the left of a veterinary clinic. Cross Westbrook Road and walk ahead to Church Street. Keep forward past the entrance of St. Peter & St. Paul's church on your left taking the narrow path with the graveyards and allotments on your left. After passing the allotments, with fine views across the Lammas Lands to the left, cross over the road into the large Crown Court car park.

1. Leave the car park and proceed to the High Street between the public conveniences and the Wetherspoons public house. On reaching the High Street, turn left and then first right into Queen Street. At the top of Queen Street, cross Flambard Way using the pedestrian crossing and walk up Upper Queen Street and turn right at the top into Croft Road. Walk along Croft Road until you reach Butts Lane on the left and proceed up this narrow lane. On reaching Summerhouse Road continue forward past a road on the left until you reach the wide entrance (ignore the small alleyway beside the wide entrance) on the left into Holloway Hill Recreation Ground.

2. Pass diagonally left across the grassed area, skirting the cricket outfields, with the tennis courts and bowling green on your left. On passing the bowling green, a narrow path on the left takes you into Grosvenor Road through the gap in the wall ahead. At the far end of the road, cross Crownpits Lane into a footpath ahead and keep going to the end where it meets a crossroads. Turn left into The Drive and walk to the end, passing St. Edmund's School on your left.

3. Cross over Brighton Road using the pedestrian crossing by Busbridge Parish Church, turning right to walk up Brighton Road until you meet a bridleway/track at Heath Lane on the left, just past Busbridge School and on the right of Busbridge Village Hall. Proceed up Heath Lane going to the right at a fork, passing Gertrude Jekyll's old home, Munstead Wood, until you meet a road. Cross over into Alldens Lane and after a short distance reach a bridleway on your right. Go along this path until you meet crossing paths and here turn left just before you reach the road and, with a wooden fence on your right, proceed until you reach another road. Turn right for about 50m/55yards before turning left on to a bridleway. (There is a small wood on your right with good views between the trees which is a good point for a break).

4. Continue on this bridleway to a cross path and here keep straight ahead until you cross over a road. Carry straight on for about 1¼km/1mile, mainly downhill, with the footpath becoming a minor road. When you reach the T-junction with houses opposite, and the Old Cider House on your right, turn right and walk along the road with houses on your left and a field on your right. The road becomes a track, which curves to the right and when you meet a bridleway (to the left of the track), leave the track and walk

up a small incline when you will see some fine views on your left. The path then meets another crossing path. Turn left and keep bearing left down a slight hill and follow the path for 800m/¹/₂mile until you cross a bridge over the river Wey.

5. After crossing the bridge turn immediately left and follow the towpath, with the river on your left, back into Godalming. On the way you will cross over a road and there is a café 'Hector's on the Wey' on the other side of the river behind the boathouse. When you reach the main road by the United Church, turn left along the pavement over the Town Bridge and cross over by the central bollard. Proceed on the right side of the library with the river on your right. To return to the Crown Court car park, just before you reach the bowling green turn left and follow on, past the children's playground, over the road and through a gap in the wall back into the car park. **To return to the railway station** *keep ahead on reaching the bowling green to pass the Jack Phillips memorial and reach Borough Road. Cross this to continue along Vicarage Walk opposite and a little left. Cross the next road and walk across the station car park and up the steps.*

Circuit B (via Eashing) 7km/4¹/₄miles

6. With your back to the High Street leave Crown Court car park, go through the gap in the wall at the bottom left hand corner of the car park. Cross over the road and walk to the left past the allotments on your right and on through the churchyard keeping the church on your left. On reaching a busy road, cross over and continue along Vicarage Walk opposite. Turn right when you reach the road and continue under the railway bridge. Then turn immediately left into New Way. **To join this section of the walk from Godalming railway station**, *come out of the main entrance bearing left to the car park entrance. Go down steps immediately on your right to the lower car park. Cross this to reach Westbrook Road and turn left. Note Vicarage Walk on your right which is the point to which you will return at the end. However, continue forward under the railway arch and turn immediately left into New Way.*

7. Walk ahead alongside the railway line going past the station platform. Ignore the footpath that leads downhill at a right hand bend and, when the metalled road curves round to the right, go ahead through some wooden posts set in the ground. Follow the footpath slightly uphill, past Ockford Wood Farm. Continue for 800m/¹/₂mile before reaching the road at the end of Halfway Lane.

8. At this point, turn right and walk carefully along the road (which can be busy at times) turning a sharp left bend by Eashing Farm on the right. Continue ahead until you reach a footpath to the right just before the first house after Eashing Farm. Proceed almost immediately over a stile and straight across a field until you reach another stile. Carry on down the hill, meeting the River Wey on your right and go forward until you reach the road. (The Stag public house is 200m/220yards ahead.)

9. Turn right and walk over the Eashing Bridge (a medieval double bridge) and before you reach the A3 turn right onto the bridleway through Greenways Farm and Stables. Proceed along the bridleway until you go through the gate ahead where the concrete roadway bears left. Keep going straight on for 800m/½mile when you will meet a cross path. (If you turn left at this point The Squirrel Inn is a five minute walk up a minor road).

10. Turn right and after 50m/55yards walk through a gate to the left of a house, Milton Wood. Continue for about 400m/¼mile with the river later appearing to your right. Reach the end of the path at Peperharow Road. Turn immediately right onto a path beside the first house. Proceed downhill and over the bridge at the bottom and turn left. Continue until you reach a T-junction. Turn right here and walk on until you pass over a roadway and through metal barriers by Westbrook Mills before meeting Borough Road.

11. Turn right along the pavement, go under the railway bridge, and then turn immediately right on to the footpath through the gap in the wall and proceed through the car park and over a wooden river bridge until you reach the end of the path. *To return to the station continue along the road a short way and turn right along Vicarage Walk. Cross the next road to go into the station car park and up the steps on the far side.* To continue to the Crown Court car park cross over Borough Road and walk along the footpath straight ahead, past the Jack Phillips Memorial on the left. Turn right at the bowling green and continue past the children's playground. Go over the road and through the gap in the wall back into the Crown Court car park.

7 From Iron Age to Space Age in the Surrey Hills – Ewhurst, Pitch Hill, Holmbury Hill and Forest Green

Cynthia's walk

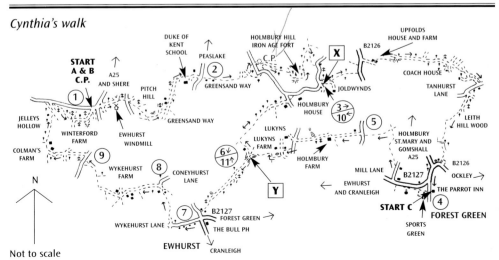

Not to scale

Length: One long walk **A**: 18^1/$_2$km/11^1/$_2$miles (sections 1-9) with two shorter versions **B**: 13km/8miles (sections 1, 2, 10 and 6-9) and **C**: (from a different start) 9^1/$_2$km/6miles (sections 4, 5, 11 and 3).

Maps: OS Landranger 187; Explorer 145 & 146.

Start: A and B: GR 074425 Hurtwood Control car park No. 4.
From Cranleigh take the B2127, Ewhurst Road. After some 800m/^{1}/$_2$mile turn left into Barhatch Road and continue on it for approximately 3^1/$_4$km/2miles. When the road rises steeply, turn left at the top of the rise and immediately left into the car park. From the A25 between Guildford and Dorking, go though the centre of Shere and continue out on Sandy Lane towards Ewhurst. When the road bends round to the right, take the left hand road over the railway. Ignore the next road on the left and continue for just over 3^1/$_4$km/2miles, then take the right fork. Look out for a minor road on the right after less than 800m^1/$_2$mile. Turn right, then immediately left into the car park.

Alternative start: C and A GR 124412 the Parrot Inn, Forest Green - park around the green. Forest Green is on the B2127/B2126 between Ewhurst and Ockley (A29) and B2126 from Gomshall (A25) and Holmbury St Mary. The Parrot Inn is just off the main roads, on the eastern side of the green facing the sports pitch. Start the walk at section 4.

Transport: Buses from Cranleigh, Horsham, Ewhurst and Dorking pass though Forest Green (start the walk at section 4). Buses from Guildford stop at the Bull in Ewhurst (start the walk at section 7 by going down Wykehurst Lane by the side of the green opposite the pub).

Refreshments: the Parrot Inn, Forest Green; the Bull PH, Ewhurst; [NB: the Windmill, marked as a PH on older maps, is now a restaurant only].

Introduction: This walk has great panoramic views from Pitch Hill and Holmbury Hill, tranquil woods, farmland and several pretty ponds along the route as well as passing the Iron Age fort at Holmbury Hill (walks A and B) and the Mullard Space Laboratory (walks B and C). Forest Green (walks A and C) is a delightful hamlet with a wide open village green measuring about 26 acres and a beautiful pond which attracts a variety of flora and birdlife. On the north side of the green is the original Smithy, now the Forest Green Forge Gallery, making ironcrafts and well worth a visit. The little village church was built by the Hensley family at the end of the 19th century as a memorial to their elder son, Ernest Charles Everard Hensley, who died in 1892 aged 18, having been accidentally shot by his cousin whilst they were out shooting rabbits. The composer, Sir Ralph Vaughan Williams, organiser and conductor at the annual Leith Hill Festival for many years, lived nearby and was an inspiration to all the local village choirs. He inherited the family home, Leith Hill House, in 1944 and gave it and surrounding lands to the National Trust.

THE WALK

Walks A and B

1. From the car park, return to the road and turn right. At the T-junction cross the road bearing slightly left to the wide track marked Greensand Way (GW) which you will now follow to the far side of Holmbury Hill. Ignore crossing paths and continue past the windmill on your right (now a private home). Turn right onto a tarred track, then take the path to the left of Four Winds, descend it with care and follow the footpath sign to the road. Cross the road and go through the gates of the car park, then go immediately right on the GW up to the top of Pitch Hill, where you can see wonderful views as far as the South Downs on a clear day. Continue along the top of the hill past the trig point, ignoring all tracks to the left, until you reach a GW marker post. Turn left along the path with an intermittent wooden rail on your right. After about 200m/220yards take a right turn at the GW marker post. At the bottom of the hill turn left by the GW marker post onto a tarred drive. Continue ahead through the metal barrier and after a few hundred metres/yards look for a GW marker post on your right. Take this track downhill and continue down the stepped path and through a kissing gate. Continue down with a fence over on your right to the Duke of Kent School grounds and walk down the drive to the road.

2. Cross the road bearing slightly left to a footpath (fingerpost - Greensand Way). This path continues over a stile and then opens up with fields on either side for about 800m/½mile. Shortly after a kissing gate (marked McKenney's Gate) bear right into woodland. At a T-junction of paths, turn left (marked Greensand Way), then at a fork take the right hand path to the road. Cross this to go uphill into a car park (GW marker post). Continue ahead and take the path on your right, immediately before the Holmbury Hill noticeboard, going between concrete bollards. Continue straight ahead down to a crossing track and over it to pick up the path on the other side. This path climbs up to an open area with wheelchair access paths and a pond on your left. Cross this area to the path in the right-hand corner and continue on this path keeping right at a wooden barrier. Keep right at all tracks until you reach the top of Holmbury Hill and the site of the recently excavated Iron Age Fort. On reaching a circular seat, take the path to your left marked with a GW post. (It is worth taking a little time first to enjoy the fantastic views from the summit and read the viewpoint and Iron Age Fort information.) Go through the wooden barrier marked 'Footpath Only' (ignoring the steep bridleway going downhill on your right), and go ahead on a permissive footpath still keeping right to join the lower path and again keeping to the right at all junctions. Carry on through light woodland mostly going downhill until you reach the next wooden barrier. Shortly after, at a waymark post on your right, take a sharp right turn down a public bridleway now leaving the Greensand Way and continue downhill until you reach the road after approximately 400m/¼mile. Turn right and continue carefully along this road until you reach Joldwynds on your left. **[Point X on sketch map] For walk B follow the instructions at section 10 before re-joining walk A at section 6.**

3. **To continue the full route A**, take the stony bridleway downhill to the left of Joldwynds and follow this through light woodland and over a stream via two railway sleeper bridges. On reaching the road turn left, taking care as there is no pavement or verge, then after about 200m/220yards turn right onto a bridleway towards Upfolds House and Farm. After the house the bridleway bears left in front of some barns, then shortly bears right. Continue for about 1km/²/₃mile to a junction of paths. Continue in the same direction, bearing slightly right, to the bridleway (marked by a fingerpost and waymarker) after the entrance to Coach House on your right. Follow the bridleway uphill, very soon taking the right fork onto a footpath at a waymarker with blue and yellow arrows. The path winds through a small wood to reach a flight of steps. At the bottom of these turn right, then very shortly turn left up more steps. Continue along the footpath, enjoying the views to your right, and on reaching the lane, turn right. Continue down the lane past cottages on your left and after about 200m/220yards, just before the lane turns sharply left, turn left into Leith Hill Wood, indicated by a sign saying 'National Trust, Leith Hill Place'. From the top of this wood to the bottom is over 1km/²/₃mile, so don't panic! **At each junction of paths you will be keeping to the right.** Go downhill on the main track until you reach an orange topped NT waymarked post where the main track bears left. Leaving the main track, carry on downhill through woods to reach a purple topped waymarker just before another main track. Turn right along the track for a short distance and then opposite another purple topped marker, turn right onto a grassy track which eventually leads to the road. When you cross a wooden footbridge there will be another 300m/330yards still to go. Turn right at the road and walk along the right hand edge, taking care as the traffic can be quite busy. As soon as you reach the pond at Collins Farm, cross to the other side of the road and continue along the path ahead through the wide grassy area parallel to the road on your right. Keep to the left at the fork in the road and you will very soon arrive at the the Parrot Inn, Forest Green.

Walk C starts here

4. With your back to the front entrance of the Parrot Inn, cross the road and take the path ahead of you across the village green, passing the sports green to your left. On the far side, take the left fork towards the cottages. Cross the first driveway, then bear left at the second driveway to join the footpath in front of the cottages. Continue to walk away from the pub, past the church until you reach the roadside. Bear left and continue on the grass verge until you are opposite Mill Lane on the right. Cross the road and continue up this lane, ignoring any side turnings until you reach Park Cottages, then take the footpath opposite on the left. In a short while, cross a stile and continue with the fence on your left. When the fence bends round to the left, go straight ahead to the marked footpath. Follow the footpath towards telegraph poles and, bearing left, keep the telegraph lines on your right until you reach a stile. Cross the stile and turn immediately left at the junction of paths to follow the footpath along the left side of the field. Cross the next stile and continue straight on across the middle of the field to a metal gate. Cross the stile on the left of the metal gate to the road.

5. Turn right up the road and very shortly turn left along a bridleway to Holmbury Farm. At the top of the rise, turn right in front of the farmhouse to follow the bridleway round. The track then bends to the left between farm buildings. After wooden barns on your left take the right fork on the bridleway going downhill, passing a pond on your right, then rising gradually to a road. Turn left onto the road and after approximately 100m/110yards, take the footpath over a stile on your right. Keep to the left of the hedge, but do admire the gardens of Lukyns on the right. Cross a driveway to the footpath on the left of a pond. Keeping the fence on your right follow this path along as it bears right (ignoring a footpath off left) then left. In another 200m/220yards there will be a metal gate on the right with a stile crossing the corner of the wooden fence. Cross the stile, then almost immediately take the footpath on the left, keeping the fence on your right, until you reach another stile at crossing paths.

Point Y – For walk C, go to additional instructions at section 11. For walk A, cross the stile and, keeping to the left, go over a concrete bridge. Walk B joins at this point.

6. Continue on the footpath with trees and a ditch on your left. As the ditch goes round to the left, continue straight ahead across the field and through a gate into woodland. Go over a farm track and continue ahead with a field on your right and continue through the woods ignoring paths to left and right. At the bottom of a gentle slope, continue ahead past a footpath waymarker sign, then go across the field to a footbridge. Cross this and continue up the next field keeping to the right. At the end of the field cross a stile, bear left and continue along a wooded path until you reach the road. Turn left down the road for about 100m/110yards to the mini-roundabout. The Bull PH is opposite.

7. Turn right along Wykehurst Lane and continue for just over 400m/¹/₄mile. After the last house on your left there is a field. Continue down the lane beside this field until you reach a metal gate at the end of it, where you take the footpath opposite on your right to go uphill through the woods. After about 200m/220yards, go over a stile between two metal gates and continue to the next stile. Go over this stile and follow the path as it goes right then immediately left (with a wooden bench on your right). Follow this wide grassy track between fences to the far end, passing a house on your left until you reach a gravelled drive. Turn right and go through the gates to a lane. This is Coneyhurst Lane.

8. Turn left into the lane and, ignoring footpaths to left and right, walk on until you reach Wykehurst Farm, where you keep to the right hand track. At the end of this track bear slightly right through a wooden gate at the junction of three paths and continue on the bridleway, with farm buildings on your right. Keep on ahead ignoring the path on your left. The path soon turns sharply right. Continue on this bridleway for about 400m/¹/₄mile, ignoring two footpaths off to your right, crossing a footbridge, until you reach a road.

9. Turn right to go up the hill on the road and then left at a bridleway fingerpost towards Winterfold Farm. After about 400m/¹/₄mile, immediately before Colman's Farm house and Winterfold Farm, follow the track round to the left. At the T-junction of bridleways, turn right, then take the right fork. Continue gradually uphill and at the next fork take the path on the right (this path is usually in better condition than the one on the left, but they soon rejoin each other). Then after a very short distance at the next fork keep left. Go past Jelleys Hollow cottage on your left, keeping ahead on the bridleway, and continue going uphill, eventually to join a road. Turn right, then in about 30m/33yards follow the GW footpath on the right (fingerpost), parallel to the road. This path climbs slowly uphill. Turn right at the first crossing path, away from the road, then fork left, and then immediately fork right. At a T-junction of paths, turn right and continue on the main track ignoring paths on the left. Soon after a GW waymarker post, look to the right for a path through to panoramic views and stop to enjoy them. Retrace your steps to return to the GW path and continue to the right (here you will find the Lord Justice James seat on the right hand side of the path) and carry on back to the car park.

Walk B

10. As walk A, sections 1 & 2 until point X on the sketch map. Ignore the bridleway and continue along the road, passing the entrance to Holmbury House on your left, once owned by the Guinness family, but now the Mullard Space Science Laboratories, part of University College London (ignore the footpath to the right of the gates as this is always extremely boggy even during spells of hot dry weather). Continue along the road past a row of pretty cottages on the right, then at the end of the brick wall on your left you will see a footpath to the left of a wooden gate ahead. Take this path and at the end cross the road bearing left, then take the bridleway on the right through a gateway and continue straight ahead past a building on the left. Where the drive starts to go uphill, take the track to the left and continue on this bridleway for about 800m/¹/₂mile through woodland and then gradually downhill. (This path can get very muddy in winter.) Shortly after the path opens up into a wide grassy track between fences, look out for a stile on the left. Cross the stile and the field ahead and go over the stile on the far side. Turn left onto a drive then right to go over a stile. Follow the path round with a fence on your left and cross the next stile. Turn right and go over a concrete bridge. **Re-join walk A at section 6.**

Walk C

11. Start at the Parrot Inn, Forest Green. Follow sections 4 and 5 to point Y on the sketch map, then cross the stile and **immediately bear right**, crossing the second of two adjacent stiles on your right. Follow the path round with a fence on your right, go over the stile, bearing left on a farm driveway to a stile on your right. Go over this stile and cross the field to a stile with a bridleway waymarker post. Cross the stile and turn right. Follow this track uphill for approximately 800m/¹/₂mile to a road. Cross the road, bearing slightly left to a footpath opposite on the right. Go along this footpath and at the end turn right at the road. Continue along the road past a brick wall on your right, ignoring the footpath on your right as this is usually very boggy, even during spells of very dry weather. Go past a row of pretty cottages on the left. You will soon pass the entrance to Holmbury House, now the Mullard Space Science Laboratories, part of the University of London, on your right. Continue for another 200m/220yards or so until you reach Joldwynds on the right, **point X on the sketch map. Finish the walk by following section 3 of walk A.**

8 In Hampshire Hanger and Gilbert White country – Alton, Upper Farringdon and Selborne

Julian's walk

Length: 20km/12¹/₂miles.
If using the bus (see below) for the outward/return journey, the walk can be shortened; it is 9¹/₂km/6miles from Alton to Selborne, 10¹/₂km/6¹/₂ miles from Selborne to Alton.

Maps: OS Landranger 186; Explorer 133.

Start: GR 720392 the entrance to Coors Brewers Limited, Lower Turk Street, Alton, beside a railway bridge. From the A31 follow directions to the town centre and follow the main route to reach Drayman's Way, where both car parks will be found. If coming from Selborne, you will pass Lower Turk Street before reaching the car parks on your left. Parking is available close to the start at Manor car park GR 718393 or Rogers Court car park GR 719394. To reach the start from the car parks, turn right along Drayman's Way to a mini roundabout, turn left into Lower Turk Street beside the Brewery.

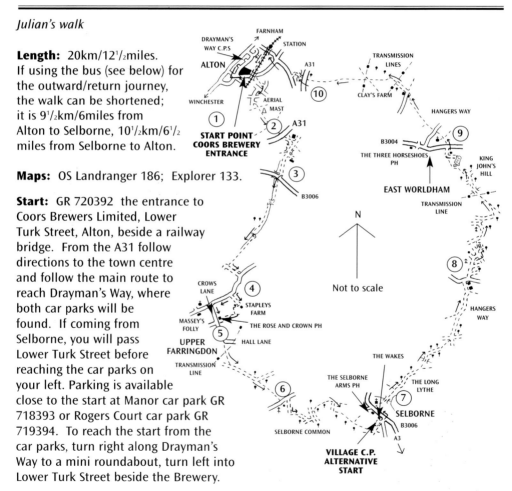

Alternative start: GR 743335 Selborne Village car park. Follow the B3006 into Selborne from either the A31 or A3. The car park is just off the High Street with entry from the minor road beside the Selborne Arms. Start the walk at section 7.

Transport: Alton railway station is the terminus of the London Waterloo/Woking/Alton line. To reach the start, leave the station car park area on the north side of the track by the Hangers Way sign and on crossing the main road, turn up a flight of steps by the railway bridge, marked to 'Lower Turk Street and Brewery (480m)'. Follow this path parallel to the track until you reach another main road, Lower Turk Street, with Coors Brewery entrance on your right. Buses from Farnham to Winchester or Alton to Selborne stop in the High Street, or Drayman's Way. There is an option of doing half the distance either just as far as Selborne or just back from there to Alton, by using the local bus service for the return journey.

Refreshments: the Rose and Crown PH, Upper Farringdon; the Selborne Arms PH; the Queens Hotel, Bush House and the Tea Parlour at Gilbert White's House, all in Selborne.

Introduction: I find this a really enjoyable walk through fields and woods with wide open views at times. Some of it follows the Hangers Way (hangers are the richest woodland on English chalk – a series of steep sided wooded hills) so there are some hills along the route! Two interesting churches at Upper Farringdon and Selborne can be visited as well as The Wakes, the house of naturalist Gilbert White and the Oates Museum, in Selborne. It is probably best walked in the spring and summer months when it is likely to be less muddy.

THE WALK

1. From the Brewery entrance, go under the railway bridge and immediately turn right up a steep flight of steps across the road at the point where Lower Turk Street becomes Ashdell Road. Follow this path upwards and on reaching a T-junction of paths, turn left into a residential road. Turn right and then right again out of Vaughans into Crowley Drive. At a T-junction, turn right and then shortly left up The Ridgeway. Carry straight on and at the bottom of a hill turn left into Salisbury Close. Almost immediately bear right up a tarmac path across a grassy area (opposite Sandown Close) towards an aerial mast. Go through a kissing gate and follow the footpath marked ahead towards the middle of a belt of trees. Keeping the aerial mast to your left, go through a gate with a plaque on it saying that it was donated and erected by members of the Alton Ramblers Association. Pass the brick building above you on the right and continue on towards the gate in front of you.

2. Emerge into a field with broad views to the south and go straight ahead to a stile in the hedge line. Cross this and carry on straight ahead over the next field and down to a kissing gate. Go through this to the corner of a lavender field and follow the footpath straight ahead down the left field edge towards a main road at the bottom. Cross over a stile and go down steps to the A31. Taking care on this busy road, cross over slightly diagonally left to the fingerpost below the flight of steps. Go up these into a field. Go through a kissing gate and continue straight ahead, keeping a fence and buildings to your left, to a T-junction. Turn right along a tarmac drive with a pretty stream flowing alongside left. Cross a bridge with brick parapets and keep ahead on the tarmac drive, ignoring a footpath off right and a drive up to a house on the left. Continue past a wall built from local stone, and stay on this drive for about 800m/¹/₂mile to reach the Alton/Selborne road (B3006).

3. On reaching the main road, turn right for a short distance (no verge, so take care here) and then turn left onto a footpath just before the road crosses a stream. Continue straight ahead to cross a stile, keeping parallel with the overhead cables to your left, then bear slightly left under the power line keeping the stream to your right and the hedge/tree line to your left. On reaching the fence ahead of you, turn right as directed by the fingerpost, cross a plank bridge and turn left over the stile by a fingerpost. Head roughly straight ahead, keeping a fence on your right, and keep forward as the field narrows, passing a strip of woodland on your right. Level with the end of this woodland, go over a grassy bridge on your left to cross a tiny stream (the Caker) and turn right, now following the stream on your right. Cross over a stile and keep forward in the next field, with the small stream over to your right and cross another stile at the end of the field onto a broad grassy track. Reach a T-junction with a well maintained crossing track and turn left on this to reach a small lane (Gaston Lane).

4. Turn right along the lane where Upper Farringdon church spire is in view ahead right.

Should you wish to visit the church, continue along the lane for 800m/¹/₂mile, noting Crows Lane on your left. The 800 year old church of All Saints, where Gilbert White, the naturalist from Selborne, was curate is on the right and has a 3,000 year old yew tree in the churchyard. Almost opposite and reached via the lych gate on the far side, is the interesting brick and terracotta tiled building called Massey's Folly, a regional runner-up in the BBC Restoration Village series in 2006. It was the creation of the local vicar and eccentric, the Reverend Thomas Hackett Massey, being intended originally to house a new religious order. It was begun in 1870 and eventually completed in 1925, six years after his death. To rejoin the route, retrace your steps as far as Crows Lane and turn right along this to the Rose and Crown pub and a road junction. Keep forward along Hall Lane and continue at section 5.

Follow the lane for about 500m/550yards and turn left by a fingerpost along a track towards Stapleys Farm. Just before the house note a fingerpost in the hedge left and turn sharply right to pass between a hay barn left and a shed right and reach a stile. Keep straight on along the bottom edge of a field to cross a stile hidden in the corner. In the next field turn left keeping the hedge on your left, and cross another stile. At this path junction turn right alongside a wire fence and follow this, turning left at the top along the field edge and soon reaching an opening to the garden of The Rose and Crown pub. Here bear right down a footpath alongside a brick wall to emerge beside a thatched house at a road junction. Turn left and walk up Hall Lane.

5. Follow Hall Lane going gently uphill and later passing Upper Farringdon House on your left. Leave the road at a left hand bend to take a footpath on your right going diagonally uphill across a field and under a power line. Reach a bridleway where you can turn round to enjoy the wide ranging views to the north. Turn left along what can be a slightly boggy section, continue straight ahead past field openings and where the bridleway bears round to the left in trees, peel off straight ahead on a footpath with a yellow waymarker. Note the line of the path indicated by the arrow (which maintains your previous direction), and follow this diagonally across the field to a stile down the slope in the tree line. Cross this and continue diagonally downhill on a slightly overgrown narrow path to start off with, to reach a stile at the bottom. Go over this and head down across a field towards woodland to cross another stile out into a lane.

6. Turn left along the lane, and shortly turn right onto a broad track going over a stile by a gate. Immediately before the track heads out into a field, turn left up the footpath beside the tree line, with good open field views now to the north-east. Bear right over a stile back into woodland and keep forward along the left-hand path close to the field edge on your left. At a T-junction with blue topped marker posts, turn left downhill and at the next marker post keep left with the field still on your left. On reaching a fingerpost turn right sharply downhill signed 'Permitted Horse Route'. At the foot of the hill, turn left between two fields then bear left with the field on your left and keep left at next fork. Continue on this track until the point where the track leaves the wood and you reach a National Trust (NT) sign 'Selborne Common' on your right. Here turn right uphill on a path and very shortly branch left so that a field boundary fence is immediately on your left. Continue on this path with views of Selborne on your left. Ignore the stile on your left and continue forward with a view of The Wakes (Gilbert White's House) across the field to the left until you reach another NT sign 'Selborne Common' with an information board. This is the bottom of the zig-zags cut by Gilbert White and his brother. Turn left down a fenced path into the village of Selborne.

If starting the walk from Selborne, turn left out of the car park and go down towards the main street.

7. Turn left in the village passing the Selborne Arms on your left and head on up the main village street towards the Selborne Gallery in front of you. Turn right here onto the Hangers Way (which you follow for much of your return route) marked to Alton and go through a gate into the churchyard. If you have time take a look inside the 800 year old church at the stained glass windows commemorating Gilbert White and look for his grave. Go through the gate at the other end of churchyard, and follow the path on downhill towards a red-tiled roofed cottage in the distance. Go over a footbridge, signed 'Hangers Way', and follow the path, ignoring a marked path to your left, before entering NT woodland called The Long Lythe. Eventually you emerge out into an open field with a lake to your right. Bear to the left following the fencing to a corner and a small metal gate, then turn right following Hangers Way markers, heading towards a plank bridge over to a stile. Cross this, bear left uphill towards the tree line on your right, cross a stile by a gate and go out onto a broad track into woodland. Emerge into another open field and head round to your left at first towards a fenced pond, then keep forward across the slope, heading for a stile in the tree line on the far side. Cross this and turn left onto a track in the woods which are carpeted with flowers in spring. Ignore a path immediately bearing off right and carry on up the main track, eventually coming down to the thatched Candovers Barn on your right and further houses after that. Continue, now on a metalled road, past High Candovers to a T-junction where you turn right downhill, soon turning left onto a path and still following signs for the Hangers Way.

8. Continue straight ahead through woodland, at first walking parallel with the field fence on your left and ignoring two turnings off right downhill into the wood. You are still following Hangers Way markers. At the next junction turn right, following a Hangers Way sign directing you downhill towards a surfaced track. On reaching this, turn left as marked and shortly bear off right as marked onto a narrow footpath that skirts the pond to your left. You soon come to a convenient spot for a break provided by a few tree stumps. Keep forward where a path round the other side of the pond joins from the left and reach a T-junction with a main forest path. Turn right down to a kissing gate and into a field. Bear diagonally left to another obvious kissing gate in the tree line. Continue straight ahead on a broad grassy path in woodland, using alternative paths to the right of this to avoid any particularly muddy stretches. Where the broad path swings sharply left, keep forward on the narrow path marked as the Hangers Way. Soon you reach a T-junction of paths where you turn right and shortly go through a gate into a Woodland Trust area. Now bear left in this open area following the tree line as marked. Continue ahead keeping the fence on your left and following a fairly distinct path over the grass. Keep forward through an overgrown section with brambles, passing an open grassy area to your right, and cross a plank bridge and kissing gate ahead into an open field. Follow the direction of the fingerpost and bear diagonally left, going under the overhead power lines to a railed footbridge in the hedge. Cross this and continue diagonally to the next kissing gate. Go through this and continue straight ahead uphill on a broad green track. At a T-junction turn left onto another broad green track. Go through another kissing gate and proceed straight ahead on a flat green tree-lined track in the field, following it downhill to a lake. Bear left and go across short plank bridge to a gate. Turn diagonally right heading uphill towards another gate on the far side of the field, to the left of farm buildings. Here there are excellent views back behind you to King John's Hill. Go through the gate and bear right up the drive with trees to your left and a farmhouse and farm buildings to your right, to reach a main road (B3004).

9. At the main road, briefly leave the Hangers Way and cross over to a marked footpath directly opposite which goes through a gate in the fence of The Old School House. Proceed ahead on a very narrow path beside a fence to your right leading up to a stile. Across this, turn left to walk steeply uphill then go through a gate leading out into a field. Keep to the left field edge by a wire fence, passing a stile and East Worldham church and continue to a lane. Cross this and rejoin the Hangers Way by proceeding straight ahead into a field. There are excellent views in all directions along this stretch. Keep to a well used path past a footpath sign, heading towards farm buildings and an oast in the trees in the distance. When you get to the field boundary, turn right and bear left past a house, a converted hop kiln, to a lane where you turn right. After passing Clay's Farm on your left, immediately bear round to the left beside it and cross a stile or go under a barrier, proceeding up the track ahead of you, marked as the

Hangers Way, which is fenced on the left further up. Emerge into a field and go forward, ignoring the marked track off to the right and immediately pass under overhead power lines to keep ahead on a broad track through the field to the tree line. Proceed left as marked by the fingerpost now walking alongside the tree belt. After going around a bend to the right, immediately bear off left across the field to an isolated fingerpost in the dip. On reaching this, continue forward under a further power line; ignore a crossing path and eventually cross into another field by a fingerpost and follow the left field edge. Cross over a stile in the far left corner of the field and one further stile just around the corner underneath another power line. Continue straight across a field to go over a stile to the left of a pylon out to the A31.

10. Cross the road very carefully, to the Hangers Way sign on the other side of the crash barrier and proceed down to cross a further stile and then a footbridge. Bear round to the left as the track becomes gravelled, going uphill to a road and keep ahead uphill out to the main road junction. At this point, turn right as marked, along the Hangers Way towards Alton town centre. Keep to the main road and at a staggered crossroads, go straight on downhill into Paper Mill Lane and under the railway bridge. **If returning to the station**, cross the road and shortly turn right up the path into the station car park. **If going to the car parks**, immediately turn left up a flight of steps marked to 'Lower Turk Street and Brewery (480m)'. Follow this fenced path, with a wall to your right and the railway line to your left and at a footpath sign on the left, turn right between houses. Continue straight ahead past a small parking area on your left and carry on up to a factory building ahead of you where you follow the road round to the left past houses towards the main inner by-pass road, Drayman's Way. Proceed left along this to the car parks.

On the heathland of Elstead, Thursley and Hankley Commons

Denis and Susan's walk

Length: A figure of eight walk: total length 18km/11¼miles with a walk, Circuit A, to Elstead of 10km/6¼miles, (sections 1-8) and another, Circuit B, to Thursley of 8km/5miles (sections 9-14).

Maps: OS Landranger 186: Explorers 145 and 133.

Start: GR 899416 the Moat car park, Thursley Road, Elstead.
From the A3 take the B3001 to Elstead; at the village green, take the road on the left towards Thursley and Churt. The Moat car park is on the left after about 2½km/1½miles.

Alternative starts: GR 907437 roadside parking at Elstead village green and opposite the village hall (join the walk at the end of section 6 by turning into Stacey's Farm road).

or GR 900397 Thursley village recreation ground car park area (start at section 13.) From the A3 take the exit to Thursley and drive into the village passing the pub, the village hall and the turning left to the church. The recreation ground and car park are on the right.

or GR 891411   Ministry of Defence (MoD) car park on Hankley Common (see instructions at start of section 10). From Elstead village green take the road to Thursley and Churt, pass the entrance to the Moat car park on your left and continue until you reach a double bend by Truxford Riding Stables where you turn right onto a small MoD road. Drive uphill for about ³/₄km/¹/₂mile; the car park is on the left at the top.

Transport: Buses from Aldershot, Farnham, Godalming and Guildford pass though Elstead.

Refreshments: the Woolpack PH, the Golden Fleece PH and the Mill at Elstead; the Three Horseshoes PH, Thursley.

Introduction: This is a heathland walk, usually dry underfoot except perhaps for the fields from Elstead village which can be muddy in wet weather. The terrain is gently undulating, with extensive views across open heather-covered slopes, richly purple in late summer. Boarded walks lead across the wetland bog of Thursley Nature Reserve, famous for its dragonflies as well as rare plants and birds, which was badly burned in a fire in the hot summer of 2006 but is gradually regenerating. Close to the path on Hankley Common is the Atlantic Wall, a large

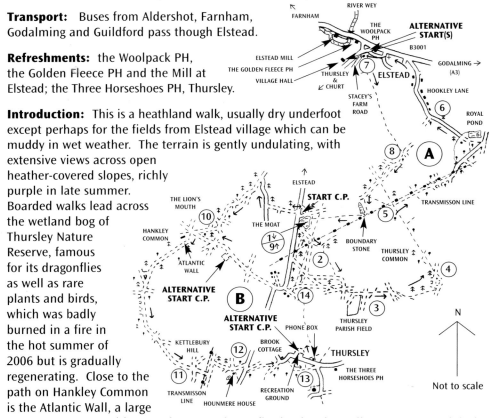

concrete structure with an explanatory plaque fixed to it. The Wall was constructed during World War II for Canadian troops who used it in training for the invasion of France. The pretty village of Thursley, with its church, is worth a detour from the village green.

THE WALK

Circuit A (via Elstead/Thursley Common) 10km/6¹/₄miles

1. Starting at the Moat car park, take the path from behind the Nature Reserve notice board to the lake. Turn left and follow the narrow path round to the right, skirting the lake and crossing a footbridge. On reaching an open sandy area, ignore a narrow path forking left and continue forward between trees, leaving the lake behind. After about 75m/80yards take a left fork towards open ground to reach a sandy bridleway. Cross over and continue ahead onto Thursley Nature Reserve, passing beneath power lines and onto a boardwalk. Follow this, to emerge onto a wider track with an 'EN Heath Trail' marker post.

2. Turn right along this track, with the bog on the right and open heath on the left. After a short stretch of boardwalk, at a T-junction and an EN (English Nature - now part of Natural England so markers may change) marker post, turn left onto a narrow path between gorse bushes. Continue forward for about 100m/110yards, and at a T-junction and another EN marker post, turn right to a wide sandy track. Cross straight over to go slightly uphill on a wide track. After about 50m/55yards look for an indistinct path on the left through woodland, soon passing the fenced area of Thursley Parish Field on the right. The track bears left, leaving the Field at a waymark post and crossing track.

3. Continue ahead along a sandy path which becomes stony, through open heathland, going gently uphill to reach a wide sandy crossing track at a waymark post. Cross the track to another post and take the left fork through heather, leading uphill to pine trees. Through the pine trees the path leads downhill to join a sandy track from the right at a waymark post. Bear left along this for a short distance to a waymark post at a crossing track, go forward on a wide track through pines and quickly over another crossing track to a waymark post with a yellow footpath arrow on your left.

4. Follow this footpath, indistinct at first but marked by white arrows painted on the pine trees, soon to emerge onto open heathland, crossing an indistinct bridleway at a waymark post. Continue ahead on a very straight path for about 1¼km/¾mile, following yellow arrow signs and white posts, crossing a wooden footbridge and going over a short stretch of boardwalk to a T-junction at a bridleway with a waymark post.

5. Turn right, to go across reclaimed heathland that can be soggy in places, passing an EN map-board, to a waymark post at a bend in a broad gravelled track. Continue straight ahead on this, which becomes metalled, with fields on the left and bearing right over a bridge. Look for a waymark post with a yellow footpath arrow on the left, shortly before Royal Pond. Follow this narrow path through trees to emerge onto open grass by a cottage and buildings. Cross to the gravel driveway and continue through the gateway on a metalled road to the end of Hookley Lane, with houses on the right.

6. Follow Hookley Lane to the main road (B3001) through Elstead. Turn left, and just past the United Reformed Church, turn left into Springfield then right into Back Lane to reach the village green by the Woolpack public house. (Also close by for refreshments are the Golden Fleece and Elstead Mill, on the road towards Farnham.) Keep left with the road signposted to Churt/Thursley and shortly after passing the Spar shop, turn left into Stacey's Farm Road. Immediately turn left behind a stone wall, onto a narrow path going steeply uphill beside a house and garden, to a stile into a field.

If parking around the Green or opposite the Village Hall, join the walk by turning into Stacey's Farm Road and following the footpath uphill.

7. Go through the kissing gate and follow a hedge on the left, with views of Elstead on the right, to a second kissing gate and a crossing path. Continue ahead through fields, over stiles (some no longer in use) and with a hedge on the right until the path bears left to reach a metal gate and stile into another field. At the bottom of this field, ignore the stile ahead and turn right onto a bridleway going through woodland.

8. Emerging onto a gravelled track, turn left, then immediately right onto a waymarked bridleway between tall pine trees, following the parish boundary line on the left. After passing a waymark post, continue on a sandy track, crossing another bridleway to reach an EN National Nature Reserve board on open heathland. Here turn left onto a narrow path winding between pine trees marking the parish boundary, to reach a boardwalk round Pudmore Pond. The boardwalk turns right at a boundary stone marking the parishes of Elstead, Peperharow and Thursley. Continue ahead, ignoring a boardwalk to the left, to exit at a crossing bridleway by an EN notice board. Still going ahead, follow the path between trees and shortly turn right at a T-junction to skirt the Moat on the left, and back to the car park.

Circuit B (via Thursley) 8km/5miles

9. From the car park, exit to the road and cross slightly right to the fingerposted footpath opposite. Follow this to a metalled road and opposite a driveway to Elstead Manor. Turn right and at a right hand bend in the road turn sharp left at a waymark post for bridleway 108, a wide track with woodland on the left and a fence on the right, then open heathland. On reaching more woodland and a waymark post, now on the MoD land of Hankley Common, ignore the track going right and continue ahead beneath pine trees, ignoring other tracks, until you reach an open area and a junction of several tracks. Turn right onto a track exactly opposite a waymark post on the left indicating bridleway 108. Follow this uphill continuing to another open area, known as the Lion's Mouth with fencing (bridleway 101) to the left.

To join the walk from the MoD car park return to the metalled roadway and turn left to follow this to the bottom of the hill where it swings left. Here keep forward onto a sandy track, marked bridleway 101. Follow this, later alongside fencing on the left, and keep bearing left to come to the open area known as the Lion's Mouth, joining the main route near the start of section 10.

10. Bear left and follow the left fork uphill on a rutted sandy and stony track. To the right of this track is the Atlantic Wall. At the top of the slope, passing another waymark post for bridleway 108, is a wide vista of a horseshoe-shaped bowl, with MoD army huts below at the mouth. This area is much used by the army today and has been used in the past for parachute training, hence its name of the Dropping Zone (DZ). Bear right and follow the wide track round the rim of this bowl along Kettlebury Ridge. After about 1½km/1mile, passing three waymarked tracks on the right, reach open country with heather slopes on both sides and take an obvious track, forking left, to the summit of a small hill, a good place for a rest. This is Kettlebury Hill and is one of the highest points of the Commons, giving an extensive view of the Hog's Back from Guildford to Aldershot, with the radio mast of Crooksbury Hill an obvious landmark.

11. From the hilltop, facing away from the valley, take the left hand fork down to rejoin the ridge track at a junction with several other tracks. Go straight ahead along a narrower track between overhanging pine-trees, skirting a slight dip which is often flooded. Follow this sandy level track to arrive beneath crossing power lines. Turn left to follow the power lines downhill, sometimes steeply. At the bottom turn right onto a grassy track with a fenced-off conservation area on the left, arriving at a narrow metalled road and exiting MoD land. Keep ahead, passing Hounmere House on the right and bear left uphill to reach a road.

12. Turn right and, taking care of passing traffic, after about 100m/110yards cross to a footpath by a traffic 'bend' sign. Follow this path between a field fence on the right and laurel hedge on the left, then downhill over a wooden footbridge and in a gully to a small open field with a stream. Keep left, following the fence-line, with good views of Dye House on the left and bearing right over the stream to a stile and gate into a metalled lane. Turn left along the lane to reach a road at a bend with Brook Cottage opposite. Turn right, taking great care of traffic, to go uphill for about 75m/80yards to '30mph' and 'Road Bends' signs on the right. Behind these signs turn sharply right to take a narrow leafy path uphill between high sandy banks. Follow this path, ignoring any minor side-tracks, exiting onto a lane between old cottages and leading up to Thursley Village Green (village and church to the right; the Three Horseshoes for refreshments ahead; car parking on recreation ground to the left).

If starting from Thursley village recreation ground car park, face the road and walk to the left to reach a road junction. Turn left onto a stony bridleway (signed) opposite a grassy triangle and seat. Continue the directions in section 13.

13. Turn left to pass a seat erected for '1977 Silver Jubilee of H.M. Queen Elizabeth II' and cross the road to a stony bridleway beside a telephone box. Very shortly, this bends to the right but go straight ahead down the narrowly channelled bridleway, the Greensand Way Link, at first often hidden by undergrowth. Keep straight ahead and after a short distance continue over a crossing track, going slightly downhill, to a waymark post on the right. Turn left and almost immediately take the right fork, slightly uphill and under trees to follow this hillside path, with open heath on the right and fields below on the left. At a waymark post and a junction of several tracks, keep left on a deeply sandy track. Immediately before a cottage on the left, take a short-cut across another wide sandy track leading right onto heathland. Just beyond a wide steel gate, stop at a stone structure with a 'Welcome to Thursley Nature Reserve' panel.

14. Here turn left onto a narrow path between trees, following beneath power lines. The path soon bears left along a wide grassy track and after about 75m/80yards take the right fork, passing under more power lines and continue amongst heather, gorse and pines to eventually reach the Moat. Ignoring other tracks, keep ahead with the Moat on the left, circuiting round to the left to reach the car park.

If you joined the walk at sections 10 or 13, now go to section 9 to continue the walk back to your starting point.

10 Villages and Lanes in South West Surrey - Witley, Brook, Bowlhead Green, Sandhills, Wormley and Enton

Rosemary's walk

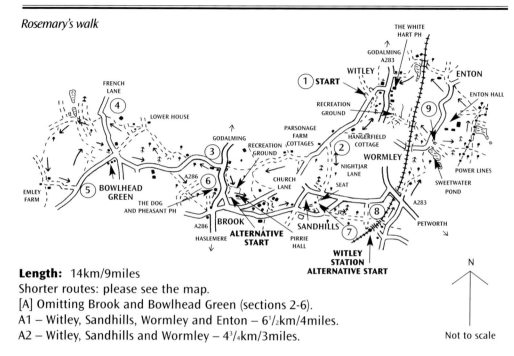

Length: 14km/9miles

Shorter routes: please see the map.

[A] Omitting Brook and Bowlhead Green (sections 2-6).

A1 – Witley, Sandhills, Wormley and Enton – 6¹/₂km/4miles.

A2 – Witley, Sandhills and Wormley – 4³/₄km/3miles.

[B] Omitting Bowlhead Green (sections 3-5).

B1 – Witley, Brook, Sandhills, Wormley and Enton – 9km/5¹/₂miles.

B2 – Witley, Brook, Sandhills and Wormley – 7¹/₄km/4¹/₂miles.

B3 – Witley, Brook and Sandhills – 5¹/₂km/3¹/₂miles.

[C] Omitting Enton (section 9).

C1 – Witley, Brook, Bowlhead Green, Sandhills and Wormley – 13km/8miles.

See also A2 and B2.

There are other variations possible but I trust these are enough to let you start exploring this little corner of Surrey.

Maps: OS Landranger 186; Explorer 133 and 145.

Start: GR 946396 Church Lane, Witley (which is opposite the White Hart on the A283, Petworth/Milford road) from the small parking area on your right by the post box just beyond the church and village school (start at section 1).

Alternative starts: GR 948379 Witley Railway Station.
or GR 930380 Brook, roadside (on A286, Milford to Haslemere road) parking alongside recreation ground, opposite the Dog and Pheasant pub (start at section 6).

Transport: Witley is on the London Waterloo/Portsmouth line (start at section 8). Guildford/Haslemere bus routes for Witley, White Hart and Witley station (start at section 8). Midhurst/Haslemere/Guildford bus route for Brook, Dog and Pheasant (start at section 6).

Refreshments: the White Hart PH, Witley; the Dog and Pheasant PH, Brook.
Note: the Wood Pigeon PH, Wormley is closed.

Introduction: This walk takes in 'sunken' old lanes, cottages and village scenes to enjoy some of the quiet spots in a very busy corner of Surrey where several roads radiate south from Milford. Helen Allingham famously painted scenes in this area and the shadow of her world of the late 19th century can still be discerned. She was one of a group of well known artists and writers of this period, living in the Witley, Brook and Sandhills area. How soon will our world also disappear with creeping urbanisation? Let's know it and enjoy it now!

THE WALK

1. From the parking area, cross the lane and go up the drive opposite marked Church Lane House. As the drive curves left, keep forward uphill on a path above the spectacularly sunken Church Lane where the exposed greensand stone is seen. The view to the left is over the Witley recreation ground with the hills around Hascombe beyond. Finally emerge onto the lane and keep forward, past Hangerfield, and continue for 400m/¼mile, passing a footpath off left immediately beside Hangerfield Cottage and later, after passing Winkford Grange on the right, note a bridleway forking off left downhill, which is known as Nightjar Lane.

[For the **shorter versions A1 and A2** turn left and follow this old bridleway right through to the road above Sandhills. You might like to digress a short way to the right along the road to enjoy the view south, before returning to take a small path directly opposite which goes down to a seat near a junction of paths. Continue from section 7 by going forward steeply down the hill.]

2. Continue up the road, passing Winkford Farm Cottages on the right, and just after the road has swung left, turn right by a bridleway sign on a drive marked '1, Parsonage Farm Cottage'. Continue to a junction of tracks by Parsonage Cottages, and keep forward on the bridleway between fields. At the end of the field on the right, ignore a path off right, and continue forward, now going at first gently downhill and then, past paths off left, more steeply downhill on an old sunken way. You have now joined the Greensand Way (GW), a wonderful 168km/105mile route following the ridge of greensand hills between Haslemere in Surrey and Ham Street, on the edge of Romney Marsh, in Kent. At the bottom reach the main A286 road.

[Those walking the **shorter versions B 1, 2 and 3** should turn in left immediately before the road, through an opening by a gate with a sign 'Heath Hills – Woodland Trust'. Keep forward on this path which is parallel with the road, continuing past a path coming in downhill left. Where the broad track swings uphill, keep ahead over a low bank on a smaller path and soon enter the recreation ground at Brook. Walk down to the road opposite the Dog and Pheasant PH. Continue the route from section 6.]

3. Cross the main A286 road carefully and go up the road opposite, past houses on the left and the wall of Witley Park right, to a lodge on the right, Pine Lodge. Here go through the kissing gate onto a steep uphill path through woodland. Continue through another kissing gate, where the path turns left and shortly, at a large crossing track turn right through a gateway to an open view across to the Hog's Back ridge on the North Downs. Keep on this broad fenced path which goes downhill and then up again to reach the next kissing gate. Cross straight over in front of the gates of Lower House and follow a path which curves left and goes over stiles and through a metal gate onto a drive near Heath Hall. Go up the steps opposite and through the gate. Turn immediately right along the field edge to a stile, go over this and bear left out to the road, French Lane.

4. Cross straight over the road following GW signs and go through a kissing gate to keep directly ahead across a field to cross stiles either side of a farm track. The path enters woodland going very steeply downhill and then bears right across a level contouring track, to continue down to another crossing track. Turn briefly right, and then go left, again steeply downhill, using old stone steps beside the remains of a wall. At the bottom, by a marker post, keep forward with a low stone wall on the right and then begin to ascend on a grassy track with a pond and garden left and Cosford Farm right. Join a metalled drive. Soon, where this bears sharply right, turn off left on an unmade cart track by a fingerpost and here you are leaving the Greensand Way. The track descends gently and as it levels out watch for a stile on the left, just by a disused gate. Cross this stile, go forward through the line of trees and then bear right to the top corner at the far end of the field to find a small metal estate gate marked P for the Pirrie estate. The path now goes up along the edge of woodland, between banks. Ignore a stile right, just before emerging at a stile straight ahead and open fields. Across this stile go diagonally right to a further stile in the corner, and join a sunken track coming up from the valley. Turn left to the top and reach a stile. There are good views here over the field gate. Turn right towards the buildings of Emley Farm and then bear round left, following the main track between the barns and this lovely old farmhouse. Follow the drive, later turning right and then left and finally reach a lane.

5. Turn left down the lane and after 150m/165yards turn in left, by a white WO marker, to a field gate. Beside this turn right through a small gate by a bridleway sign, to a second gate and then keep forward downhill beside the hedge on your right to a gate. Through this go over a crossing track and through a gate slightly left and ahead of you. Follow the sandy path downhill to the bottom with small metal gates either side. Go through the right hand metal gate and climb gently to emerge at the crossroads at Bowlhead Green. Go forward on the road towards Brook and Witley and keep left at the fork. The road begins to ascend with the wall of Witley Park running along the left hand side. Soon after it levels out, pass Uplands Stud, and after passing the entrance to Birch Copse walk a further 200m/220yards or so, then watch out for a fingerpost and steps going up the bank on the right, just before a passing place and opposite a warning triangular road sign for 'Low bridge 16 foot' ahead. Go up the steps and reach a kissing gate, then bearing slightly left, cross a field, in line with a fingerpost, to a stile on the far side. Go over this and forwards down the slope, often very overgrown, and through another small Pirrie estate iron gate. The path descends quite steeply through a line of oak trees to a further metal estate gate. Keep on downwards, beside a fence, to cross a farm track. Keep forwards over a stile to a further stile at the bottom. Directly ahead, although it may be rather overgrown, by a marker post, cross a footbridge and another stile leading into a field. Here turn diagonally left, passing to the right of an isolated oak. Near the corner of the field find a stile onto a drive and across this a kissing gate leading out to the road. Turn left and pick up the footpath around the top of the bank and follow this round to the Dog and Pheasant pub at Brook.

[**Routes B1, B2** and **B3** rejoin the walk here.]

6. Cross the road and walk across the recreation ground to the Pirrie Hall on the far side. Pass to the right of the hall and directly ahead, in the corner of the car park, go up the bank onto a footpath with gardens on the right and a strip of woodland left. Follow this to Church Lane. Turn left, go past a footpath off left, and continue to a drive on the right to 'Fintry'. Turn right up this drive, then with the garden wall in front of you, turn right through a metal gate onto a broad grassy track. Where this swings left, keep forward by a fingerpost, on a narrow path through woodland, leading down to a stile on the Sandhills Road opposite Meadow Cottage. Turn left and follow the road into Sandhills and over the crossroads with Hatch Lane and Sebastopol Lane. (Just beyond this, the parish field on the right gives fine views and has seats making it a good picnic spot.) Continue by going up the bank on the left and behind the telephone box to pick up a sandy track towards a house. Soon veer left from this up the bank to follow a path going gently uphill, keeping forward past a path off left (from which there are good views south) and reach a seat on the left.

    [**Shorter versions**. From this seat, **route B3** returns by bearing left uphill to a road, crossing straight over to a bridleway opposite, and following this all the way out to Church Lane. Here you turn right and re-trace your footsteps, turning into the footpath parallel with the lane just past the entrance to Hangerfield. **Routes A1** and **A2** rejoin the long route at this seat.]

7. Just before the seat turn right and go steeply downhill. You have now rejoined the Greensand Way (GW). Turn left on the gravel track at the bottom out to the road. Cross straight over to a fingerpost pointing along a broad track to the left. Follow this through woodland and on to Witley station, passing Pinewood Lodge on the left, and later Roberts Wood right, and continuing ahead over a small lane, by a GW marker, on a narrower stretch between fences, and finally over the footbridge near Witley station. Keep forward out to the road, opposite Hurst Cottage.

8. Turn left up the road and reach the main road (A283). Cross to the letter box and go left a short distance to turn right down an unmade drive running beside the railway track below left. Immediately past The Chestnut House, below a sign 'Private - No Through Road/No Parking/Please Turn Here', turn right onto a footpath with yellow marker, which runs alongside chestnut fencing, skirting a garden. Take care to keep beside the chestnut fencing, turning left after about 75m/80yards by a further marker post. At the end of the fencing reach a stile and across this keep ahead over a crossing path. This lovely woodland path wends along, gradually dropping downhill. Note a clearing with some large fallen tree trunks and here keep left on the main track, noting wire fencing over to your left. This main track will bring you down to walk between wire fences, with Sweetwater Nurseries over on the left, to emerge on a lane through a kissing gate. Turn right along the lane, beside Sweetwater Pond, and pass a gravelled track off right signed as a bridleway, Sweetwater Lane, and immediately beyond this reach a footpath fingerpost.

[Shorter versions. Routes **C, A2** and **B2 return** from here by turning left by a fingerpost onto a well-used footpath through woodland and continuing through a railway arch and later, by using a few stepping stones, across a small stream to emerge on a broader track. Bear right, out onto the Witley Recreation Ground and walk forward along the right-hand side towards the pavilion and the Chichester Hall. Reach and cross the road and turn right to the White Hart public house, then turn left up Church Lane to the start.]

9. Turn right by the fingerpost onto a footpath alongside the boundary of Enton Hall. Continue past the end of Enton Hall grounds and through the pine trees, on a well-used path and reach a stile. Shortly beyond this is a crossing track with a pole for carrying overhead power lines to your right. Here turn left and walk down to a double set of poles carrying power lines. Keep ahead, passing a marker post and a path coming in from the right, and now walking beneath the power lines. Keep forward through a small metal gate and along the bottom edge of a field by a depleted line of oaks, passing a pond on your right, and still following the power lines. Keep to the bottom edge and near the corner, by a fingerpost, avoid the path at the extreme edge going down to the cottage, but take the middle path which leads through the hedge and across a drive to go through a kissing gate. Turn diagonally left up the field to find another kissing gate and continue half left on a well-worn track across the next field to a stile. Follow the fenced path down to a road. Cross straight over to a letter box and track opposite. Follow this down to a junction of tracks and turn left in front of Enton Braes, on the corner, and a recent barn conversion, Cold Comfort Barn. Keep on this track as it drops down, goes under the railway bridge and comes to the pond in front of Enton Mill. As the track crosses the weir and before it swings round to the right, turn up left to a field gate and go through a small gate at the side to cross a field to the far corner and another small gate. Turn right on a wooded path leading out to the main A283 road. Cross with great care and turn left to reach Church Lane opposite the White Hart public house. Turn up the lane (you can go up the steps and through the churchyard if preferred) to return to the car park.

11 Greensand, a garden and glorious views – Hascombe, Dunsfold, Chiddingfold and Vann

Muriel's walk

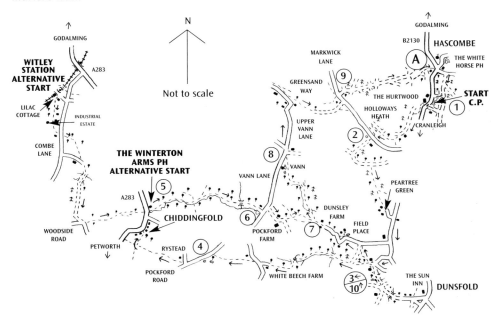

Length: 15km/9¼miles (sections 1-9) with a shorter version of 10km/6¼miles (sections 1, 2, 10, 7-9). Should you want a refreshment stop at Dunsfold, the round trip is a further 2km/1¼miles on either walk. Starting the walk from Witley station adds 3km/1¾miles each way to whichever route you follow.

Maps: OS Landranger 186; Explorer 133 and 134.

Start: GR 002391 Hascombe permissive car park opposite the Old Rectory, 400m/¼mile south of the White Horse PH on the B2130 Godalming/Cranleigh road.

Alternative starts: GR 948379 Witley railway station. See the final sections for instructions on how to reach the route at section 5.
or GR 965364 Winterton Arms, Chiddingfold (start at section 5).

Transport: Buses on the Guildford/Godalming/Cranleigh route pass through Hascombe; alight at the White Horse PH and follow the instructions from point A in section 9 to the start. Witley station is on the London Waterloo/Portsmouth line. Guildford/Haslemere buses stop at Combe Lane near Witley railway station and near the Winterton Arms, Chiddingfold. Start at section 5.

Refreshments: the White Horse PH, Hascombe; the Winterton Arms, Chiddingfold; the Sun Inn, Dunsfold; snacks and drinks can be bought at the Post Office in Dunsfold on the village green, some 100m/110yards beyond the Sun Inn.

Introduction: This is one of my favourite walks in Surrey because the wonderful views can be enjoyed with relatively few uphill stretches. The walk traverses varied countryside with woodland, streams, farms and fields. The late 13th century church at Dunsfold is certainly worth a visit. Look out for the old yew which is thought to predate the church and the three drainage holes in the walls, secured by chains, used when the church was sluiced with water to keep it clean.

At the beginning of the 20th century Douglas Caröe used his architectural expertise both to alter Vann House and to design around it a remarkable garden (possibly with some help from his friend Gertrude Jekyll). The route passes alongside the attractive pool and woodland stream garden of Vann House. (See the National Gardens Scheme information for dates of opening).

THE WALK

Long walk 15km/9¼miles

1. Walk back towards the car park entrance and turn right onto a broad grassy track. Ignoring a grassy firebreak which crosses the path, continue for another 100m/110yards to a T-junction. Turn right on to a wide level track. Ignore the grassy firebreak after 150m/165yards and proceed to enter mature trees. Do not take the path straight ahead but follow the track downhill to the right to pass through a timber yard and bear right to reach the road (B2130). (All the above tracks are permissive paths.) Cross the road diagonally to the left and after about 20m/22yards, turn right over a stile. Follow the path between hedge and field; after 300m/330yards the path turns sharp right following the field boundary uphill. At the edge of the woodland, turn left and continue on the track keeping to the left at all junctions. The path starts to descend gently passing under a holly bush to exit the woods. Turn right at the T-junction and continue along this footpath enjoying the fine views to the south. At the end of the field, turn left and follow the path to the road (Markwick Lane).

2. Cross the road and follow the path through a metal kissing gate. The path soon becomes a wider track to reach a T-junction. Turn left along the wide bridleway. Take the first path on the right, at a fingerpost, almost at the end of the woodland. After 150m/165yards, follow the path around to the left, ignoring a small track to the right. Cross over a patch which could be muddy and bear to the right following the path to exit the wood and then go over a stile. Ignoring a footpath to the left, keep to the right of the field along the fence to cross a stile in the corner. Almost immediately cross a second stile and follow the right hand field boundary past a trough. Just by the house on the right, go over a stile and follow the drive of Peartree Cottage to the road and turn right. Follow the road until you reach a signpost. Turn right along the road to Dunsfold Church.

Detour to Sun Inn, Dunsfold (2km/1¼miles)

Should you wish for a refreshment stop before continuing the route, you can divert to the Sun Inn at Dunsfold from here. With the lych gate behind you, turn right and follow the path downhill to a stile; cross this and continue alongside the water on your right to a gate. Here follow the footpath which goes across a bridge, turns right and then at a junction of paths, goes left over a metalled bridge. Continue up the bridleway ahead through trees, passing bungalows on your left as the track becomes a tarmac road (Mill Lane). Go straight on keeping close to the houses on your left till you reach the Sun Inn at the corner with Dunsfold Common Road. When suitably refreshed, return the way you came.

After taking time to look around the church, return through the lych gate, turn left and take the bridleway going left to walk past an old wooden barn on your right. Keeping the churchyard to your left, you will reach a fingerpost beside the hedgerow. **Continue the short walk at section 10.**

3. Ignoring the footpath to the right, keep to the bridleway with the churchyard on the left. Pass through a further two gates and into woodland where the path follows the edge. After passing through a small wooden gate turn left to pass through a five-bar gate. The path (a bridleway) turns immediately to the right to continue along the edge of the field. The path and field boundary curve gently to the right. Near the end of the field there is a waymark post. Here, as the field boundary bears to the right the path continues straight ahead across the field to pass through another wooden gate and over a small wooden bridge. The path now weaves straight ahead through the woodland soon joining a stream on the left. Pass through a wooden gate and follow the path with a fence and field to the right. The path crosses the stream by a concrete bridge. After about 50m/55yards the path starts to climb and bears round to the right. Further along the path widens and levels and leaves the midst of the woodland to continue along its edge. Pass The Barn and White Beech Farm and continue to the road. Cross the road to the right to a footpath sign. The path goes through a narrow gap between a gate and a tree and follows the field boundary to the right as it curves around gently to the left. At the end of the field, go through an old gateway onto the bridleway and turn left, shortly reaching the road (Vann Lane) through a gate.

4. Turn left onto Vann Lane. After 350m/385yards turn right at the T-junction signposted to Witley and Godalming. After 30m/33yards, just before Rystead House, turn left onto the signposted footpath. Just before the garage gate of the house turn sharp left as the path skirts around the garden. Bear right at a waymarked T-junction, soon moving into an open field following the hedgerow on the left, with a good view to the right of Hascombe Hill and then Hydon's Ball. About 20m/22yards before an oak tree, turn left through a gap in the hedge and enjoy views of Black Down. Now continue along the field boundary in the same direction as before towards the oak tree but now on the other side of the hedge. The path continues down into the corner of the field where a path joins from the left. Follow the track round to the right through a small stretch of woodland with a waymark post on the right. After a short distance ignore the path which goes to the left and go straight ahead following a path across a field. The path passes along a wooded field boundary to cross a stile into another field. Go straight ahead and then downhill to cross a stile to the left of a gate. After a short distance turn right onto the A283 where care must be taken of the traffic. The Winterton Arms public house can be reached just beyond Skinners Lane. If you visit the pub, turn left on leaving, to cross the car park and turn left again onto a footpath.

5. If you are not going to the pub, just before their car park turn right onto a footpath with a five-bar wooden gate and small adjacent gate. Then go through a metal gate following the track down into the woodland; this stretch could be muddy in places. Ignore the path (a byway) to the right over a wooden bridge and continue slightly uphill to the left. At a wooden sleeper bridge carry straight on, ignoring a path going slightly uphill to the left. Our path continues ahead with the stream to the right. This path exits the wood into the corner of the field and follows the field boundary on the left. At the end of the field cross the stream by a wooden bridge. The path continues straight ahead across the next two fields to some farm buildings. With the old buildings on the left pass through a wooden gate onto the tarmac track which soon joins the road (Vann Lane).

6. Turn left onto Vann Lane and then go right onto the bridleway at Pockford Farm. The track passes some houses on the left and a barn on the right; turn left with the track. After passing a house with a dovecote, the track bends to the right with a waymark on the left. Follow the direction of the waymark into the field. Continue straight ahead on the bridleway to the end of the field, ignoring cross paths. There is a five-bar gate here; turn right following the bridleway along the field boundary, through another five-bar gate and across another field towards the right hand hedge in the distance. About 50m/55yards from the end of the field is a gate to the right through which the short walkers come to join us. Do not go through this gate but turn sharp left to go down and across the field to the opposite corner.

7. Go through an old metal gate and across a wooden sleeper bridge. Follow the path to enter the woodland by a small wooden gate and follow the stream on your left to cross another bridge. Continue slightly uphill to reach Vann Gardens and Vann House and lake on your left. These woodlands and garden are particularly beautiful when the spring flowers are in bloom. At the end of the field, turn left through a small wooden gate to turn right on to a road, (ignoring the private road to Burgate Farm), and soon reach a junction.

8. At the junction bear right up Upper Vann Lane, passing houses to right and left before the road becomes steeper. 100m/110yards after the 'Unsuitable for Motors' sign climb the bank and pass through an opening to the right, turning right onto the bridleway signposted 'Greensand Way'. You will now follow the Greensand Way (GW) for almost all of the remainder of the route. At first, walk back parallel with the road and soon enjoy the wonderful views to the south west. After 800m/^{1}/$_2$mile ignore a footpath to the right and continue on the bridleway to Markwick Lane. Turn left and follow the road for about 100m/110yards and then turn right onto the bridleway.

9. Continue up the sunken footpath, which can be muddy in places. After joining a track from the right continue straight for about 400m/¼mile along the wide sandy path (a bridleway) across Holloways Heath ignoring all turnings. At cross paths keep straight on to where the path divides. Take the left fork. Where this path starts to descend steeply and becomes sunken, again take the GW to the right. Cross over a muddy patch by some logs and turn sharp left downhill ignoring the path which goes straight on. The GW is waymarked to the left but if you continue on for a short distance and take the wider track to the left this is less steep. Cross a stile into a grassy field where the path keeps to the right hand edge of the field. At the end of the field, go over two stiles, one after the other, and across a grassy field to the road (B2130) opposite the White Horse public house. *The road on the left hand side of the pub is a cul-de-sac leading to Hascombe Church and pond. If time allows these are well worth a visit.* **(A)** Otherwise take the metalled drive on the right of the pub (south side) curving uphill to the right. After 150m/165yards take the footpath to the right with a yellow waymark, passing left of the garage of Hascombe Place Farmhouse. Follow this sunken track for 200m/220yards, where, ignoring the uphill track, you take the right fork downhill on to a broader track between trees. After about 150m/165yards take the track to the right going downhill (this is the track at the start of the walk) back to car park.

Short Walk 10km/6¼miles

10. Follow the directions in sections 1 and 2. From the fingerpost, cross the field veering right and go over the stile behind the trees on the field boundary. Continue straight up the field with the fence on your left. At the end of the field the path makes a right angled turn to the right. Carry on up the field to cross the stile at the top. Turn left on the tarmac track enjoying the views of the Hurtwood and Hascombe Hill to the right. After passing a pond on the right, turn left ignoring the gateway to Field Place ahead. Soon cross a stile on the right and continue across the field between the trees and down the slope, bearing slightly right to cross the stile. Turn right onto the track, continue along past Duns House and go straight through Dunsley Farm gate, passing the farm on the left. Take the bridleway to the right through a lightly wooded area to reach a track and at a Y-junction go through the gateway on your right. Here we re-join the longer route. Ignoring the path to the left walk straight across the field to the far corner and continue the route directions at section 7.

To join the route from Witley station, turn right outside the brick station buildings and walk parallel to the railway line past the yard of Deborah Services Limited. At the end of the fence on your left, turn left to go through white gates to Lilac Cottage. Walk past the cottage on your left and continue on the narrow path until you emerge onto a much wider path coming in from your right. Follow this path ahead, firstly through light woodland and then between fences, until you reach an industrial estate.

Cross the tarmac entrance road and then continue on the lane ahead until you reach a stile. Go over this and bear left across the field keeping the tennis court on your right to cross a stile and turn left to a road. Cross the minor road carefully (Combe Lane) and go over the stile ahead, straight across a narrow field, and out over another stile into woods. Continue along a clearly defined path to the edge of the woods which you leave by another stile. Go diagonally left across the field ahead of you to another stile close to the left hand corner of the field. Cross this stile and the wooden bridge out into another field over a small stile. You can now see farm buildings on your right. Cross this field bearing left to leave by a stile in the corner. Following the direction of the fingerpost beside it, go over a wide grassy track to another fingerpost in the hedge to the right of the track (about 70m/75yards) where you turn right up the bank. Once over the stile at the top, keep forward but bearing slightly left over the rise and descend to a metal gate ahead. Pass through this, and go across a narrow strip of field to a stile. Go over the stile to enter woodland via a brick bridge, and follow a narrow path over another stream. Continue on this path as it widens and goes gently uphill to emerge into a field via a kissing gate. Walk ahead across three fields keeping the woods/hedge on your right, through three more kissing gates and reach a fenced track between houses. Continue on to the road (Woodside Road) where you turn left. Cross over Park Grove and carry on a short distance on the pavement until you reach a house called Crofts, where you turn left up the bank and then right to pick up a footpath. Follow this path over a stile into a field where you bear slightly right to reach another stile in the corner. Cross this and a footbridge to continue on the path crossing another footbridge and stile. Carry on to a further stile which you go over to bring you to the A283 almost opposite the Winterton Arms. Cross the main road with care and pick up the walk at section 5 by following the footpath at the right hand end of the car park.

Note.   Walks 11 and 13 both explore the areas around Dunsfold and Vann Lane. They meet/overlap at sections 11: 2, 10, 4, 8 and 13: 4, 7, 8, 3. See sketch maps.

---

12 Crossing the Border via the old railway line - Cranleigh, the Downs Link, Baynards and Rudgwick

---

Jean's walk

Length: 14¹/₂km/9miles (sections 1, 2, 4-10) with a shorter version of 9km/5¹/₂miles (sections 1-3, 8-10).

Maps: OS Landranger 187; Explorer 134.

Start: GR 073393 southern end of Wanborough Lane, Cranleigh.
This is reached from the B2127 Cranleigh to Ewhurst road. From Cranleigh, take the first turning right off the Ewhurst Road after the Little Park Hatch PH. There is parking for one or two cars at the end of the tarmac road.

Alternative start: GR 090343 Rudgwick, roadside parking on the B2128 near the King's Head PH (start at section 6).

Transport: Buses run along the B2127 between Cranleigh and Ewhurst and along the B2128 through Rudgwick.

Refreshments: the King's Head, Rudgwick is about 200m/220yards from the route. There are several pubs, tea-rooms and restaurants in Cranleigh about 1½km/1mile away. The Little Park Hatch on the Ewhurst Road is very close to the start. (NB: the Thurlow Arms PH at Baynards is up for sale as the book goes to print.)

Introduction: This is a pleasant walk through woodland, farmland and the Baynards Park Estate, over mainly level ground; there is no road walking, just a little walking on farm tracks and driveways in places. The woodland provides welcome shade for hot days and is carpeted with flowers in spring. The Downs Link path, here formerly the route of the Cranleigh to Horsham railway, connects the North and South Downs. The restored, award winning station buildings at Baynards, now privately owned, are of interest. There are views to the North and South Downs from the Sussex Border Path. You will encounter sheep, cows, horses, deer and possibly some miniature ponies towards the end of the walk. Dogs will need to be kept on a lead. Parts of the walk could be muddy in wet weather.

THE WALK

1. Take the public bridleway to the left of the 'Private Drive' sign indicating Pooh Corner, Antlers and Woodpeckers. Keep ahead on this wooded path ignoring all paths to the right and left for 1km/⅔mile when you will reach a crossing track and a waymarker post with a yellow arrow. Turn right and go over a stile into a field. Cross the field, keeping

the large oak trees on your left, towards a gate to the left of the building ahead. Go through the gate, across a narrow field and through a kissing gate, to reach a tarmac drive. Go straight over the drive to a footpath leading into woods, to bear right, and eventually reach a wooden barn on your left. Turn left here, towards a wooden gate, passing a concrete garage on the right. Go through the gate and ahead through woods, ahead also at a fork towards a wooden fence. Turn left at the fence and continue walking between fences to the B2128.

2. Cross the road carefully to a public bridleway directly opposite. Keep ahead to a concrete estate road and cross this diagonally right to a bridleway. This wooded path rejoins the estate road after a short time. Continue forward on this road ignoring a public bridleway and a bridge on the right. At the fork take the right hand drive to Vachery Farm as indicated on the fingerpost. **To continue the long walk, go to section 4.**

3. **For the shorter walk,** look for a bridleway fingerpost on the left at the next fork, just before the brick gate pillars for Stable Cottage. Follow this gravelled bridleway until you reach a turning circle round a tree and take the bridleway, indicated by a blue waymark, to the right of more brick gate pillars on the left. The wide bridleway keeps a barbed wire fence on the left for about 500m/550yards. Keep ahead ignoring a field entrance on the left. When the path narrows, keep forward passing a metal post in the middle of the track. Buildings soon come into view; the bridleway is now hedged on both sides. Pass the buildings on the right and keep ahead to a metal gate. Go through the gate - the bridleway bears left just before you reach the tarmac estate road. **(Continue the short walk from section 8.)**

4. **For the longer walk,** keep to the right of Stable Cottage towards a 15MPH sign. Follow the direction of the fingerpost (Public Bridleway) to the right on a clearly defined grassy track bearing right into woods, and go across a wooden bridge over a stream to a gate into a field. The bridleway now follows the right hand fenced boundary of the field to a wooden gate opposite where you entered the field. Go through the gate and turn right onto the farm track which shortly brings you onto the Downs Link at a bench, bearing the inscription 'Let the water heal you'; it faces a pond! Turn left onto the Downs Link and keep ahead ignoring all paths off it to reach picnic tables on your left and an information board about the Downs Link.

5. Keep ahead through a gate to pass the old station buildings on the left where there is an information board relating some of the history of the railway line and the station. Go forward to a road where you turn left on it for a short distance before turning right through a wooden gate onto a footpath, which soon passes under a brick bridge. Take the Downs Link 'footpath only' route ahead; cyclists are diverted back across the bridge to the Downs Link bridleway at this point. In a short time, the path goes to the left up wooden steps to cross two wooden bridges. Take a right turn from the second bridge and keep to the wooded path, with a wire fence on your left and shortly after you will pass a waymarker by a seat indicating the Sussex/Surrey border.

The path ends between two stiles; climb the left hand stile onto the Sussex Border Path which you will follow for about 1km/²/₃mile. Go straight ahead across the field for approximately 90m/100yards with woods on the right. There are views to the North and South Downs as you cross this field, keeping the clay pits on your right, a lovely picnic spot with some grand trees for shade if needed. After climbing a stile, keep ahead across the field through trees and then follow round the fence on your right until you reach another stile following the Sussex Border Path, as the fingerpost indicates. Cross the stile and go ahead keeping a wire mesh fence on your left until the path bears right and then left through woods to a gate and another fingerpost indicating the Sussex Border Path. Continue on this path until you reach a gate where you bear slightly right across a small field and through the gate opposite and climb the stile into a field where you now leave the Sussex Border Path.

If you wish to visit the King's Head pub or the church in Rudgwick, turn right, keep to the right hand boundary to a stile in the corner of the field, go over this to rejoin the Sussex Border Path to go left to the road. Cross over the road and turn right to the pub and church. To rejoin the walk, retrace your steps back to the stile at the end of the last section.

6. *If starting from the King's Head, go over the road, turn right, cross a minor road and opposite 'Hawkridge' turn left onto a public footpath. Continue forward to the second stile on your right and cross this into a field.* Turn left from the stile, and keeping the field boundary on the left go ahead. After approximately 225m/250yards look out for a stile on your left. Go over the stile onto a footpath with a wire fence on the left and a hedge on the right which then bears right to lead to a metal gate and stile out to a road.

7. Cross the road carefully to a stile (fingerpost – Footpath) directly opposite. Go over the stile and walk ahead between two small ponds and continue straight on, now with an ancient water filled moat behind a fence to your left. Follow the footpath ahead as indicated by the waymarks keeping close to the right hand fence, except when you have to walk around a fenced pond, till you come into a field to a metal gate and water trough on your right. Keep ahead as the path rises gently with a barbed wire fence on the right to a waymarker. Follow the path round to the right over a stile and keep to the right hand field boundary to a fingerpost in the hedge on the right. Follow the direction of the fingerpost left across the field. A fingerpost soon comes into view on the edge of the copse opposite. Go ahead bearing right through the woods past some old pheasant pens on the left. At a marker post, bear left, then left again to a junction of tarmac drives; cross the drives to a footpath opposite into woods.

Continue to follow the direction of the marker posts through the woods to a fenced path with buildings on your right. Keep ahead to the next marker post, not easy to see at the height of summer due to the vegetation, but it is there. Go ahead into the woods and over a stile into a field (fingerpost – Footpath). Keep to the right hand boundary to the next field. Keep ahead on the track to a metal water

trough. On reaching the trough, bear diagonally left towards a stiled bridge with metal railings. Go over this, and keep diagonally to the left of the first farm building and towards a metal gate to a tarmac drive. Keep ahead and right on the tarmac estate road initially with farm buildings and cottages on the right and barns on your left. Keep to this road for about 800m/¹/₂mile, passing the gated entrance to Brooklands on the left. After about 40m/45yards look for a bridleway (no fingerpost) slightly left of the road by a metal gate. Should you stay on the estate road to the gates to the B2128 you will encounter some unpleasant road walking.

8. **Resume the shorter walk here** Go ahead on this bridleway initially between laurel hedges to the B2128. Cross the road and take the public bridleway directly opposite. Keep to the right hand path and again the right hand path at the next metal gate. Follow this path for about 1¹/₂km/1mile as it wends through the woods, ignoring all paths to the right and left and any coloured fence posts until a crossing track is reached, waymarked with yellow and blue arrows.

9. Turn left onto the footpath and go over the stile and then ahead to a path between wire fences. Keep on through a gate and between a hedge and wooden fence to a wooden bridge, reaching a T-junction, where there is a 'Footpath Diversion' sign directly in front of you. Turn left to a gate and go through it keeping right along the right hand field boundary, and follow the path around the deer compound fencing on your right to a yellow waymarker and a gate. Go through the gate and keep straight ahead across the field to a stile. Over the stile keep ahead again to another stile and buildings. Go through the gate, keeping ahead towards a Tudor style house. Make for the right hand corner of the field where there is a stile and wooden planks across a ditch. Keep ahead to another stile onto a grassy path between hedges.

10. The public footpath keeps right of the gravel drive and houses to a track. Cross the track to go through a gate into a fenced path; walk the short distance to a second gate and go through this onto a tarmac drive. Go over the drive ahead, passing the sign for Slythehurst, Maple Stud and The Old Barn on your left. After about 20m/22yards, turn right over a stile and across the corner of the field to a stiled bridge. Keep straight ahead with a mesh fence over on the left to a stile-track-stile combination into a field and go straight ahead to the left hand corner of the field, to go over a stile which leads into Canfold Wood. Go straight over the first crossing track encountered in the woods. Soon after, turn left onto a grassy track for about 15m/18yards to a footpath on the right. The path through the woods brings you to a stile and tarmac drive. Turn right onto the drive and almost immediately left over a board footbridge at a yellow waymark. This path, mostly fenced with barbed wire, meanders through the woods. Ignore any paths to right or left until you reach some wooden steps down to the lane on which you started. Turn right and walk back to the starting point.

13 A triangle of villages in the Surrey Hills - Chiddingfold, Hambledon and Dunsfold

Nicky and Jack's walk

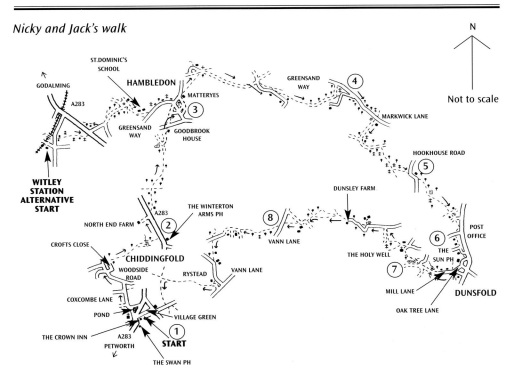

Length: 16¹/₄km/10miles.

Maps: OS; Landranger 186; Explorer 133 and 134.

Start: GR 961354 lower (southern) end of The Green, Chiddingfold close to the Crown Inn, on the A283 Witley to Petworth Road.

Alternative start: GR 948379 Witley railway station. This adds 4km/2¹/₂miles to the total distance. See instructions in the final section to join the route at section 3.

Transport: Witley is on the London Waterloo/Portsmouth line. Guildford/Haslemere buses stop at Combe Lane near Witley railway station and near both the Winterton Arms and Crown Inn in Chiddingfold.

Refreshments: the Crown Inn, the Swan PH, and the Winterton Arms all in Chiddingfold; the Sun Inn, Dunsfold; snacks and drinks can be bought at the general store in Chiddingfold and the Post Office in Dunsfold.

Introduction: This is our favourite of all the walks we can do from our doorstep. The terrain varies between woodland, farmland and pretty villages and there is some steady, gradual ascent in the first 5km/3miles. The remainder of the walk is level but still offers several extensive views. Some paths, especially at the start, can be very muddy. Bluebells and other flowers can be seen in places in late spring. There are three interesting churches on the route, at Chiddingfold, Hambledon and Dunsfold, all well worth a visit.

THE WALK

1. At the southern end of Chiddingfold Green, cross the main road with care to go right along Coxcombe Lane, between the pond and the church, until you reach the T-junction with Woodside Road. Cross over and continue to the left until the pavement ends, just after Crofts Close. Very shortly, beside a house called Crofts, take the footpath on the right and continue along by the fence and go over a stile into a field. Cross the field, bearing slightly to the right after the dip, to reach another stile in the corner. Go over this stile and a footbridge and continue ahead on the path. Ignoring a path to the right, go ahead to cross a brick footbridge and another stile and keep forward. You soon reach a stile which you go over onto the pavement by the main road (A283).

2. Turn left and walk uphill for about 400m/¼mile to the entrance of North End Farm (ignore the earlier entrance to North End). Here take care as you cross the main road and take the bridleway opposite. As the drive/bridleway bends right towards the house go left, parallel to the house and across a grassy area. The bridleway is visible ahead between the trees. Continue along the bridleway to go straight over a crossing of bridleways. Follow the bridleway for about 800m/½mile as it wends through the woods then go right at a fork, passing through some log posts. About 100m/110yards later look out for a narrow path on the right over a small wooden footbridge. Take this path which turns left to follow the edge of the woods, ignore a path to the left and emerge onto a gravel driveway. Keep ahead alongside a brick garage and Goodbrook House. The bridleway continues along the front of the house and over the grass keeping close to the fence and hedge and reaches a lane at a fingerpost. Cross over to take the bridleway nearly opposite, soon going uphill. Just past a small patch of grass on the left where the path divides, go right through the bushes onto another grassy area. Keeping close to the bushes on your right emerge onto a track and continue ahead to a lane. Cross straight over to take another track that bears left passing two garages on your left. Note the restored Well Post in the grass to your right. As the track bends round to the right, take a bridleway on the left going up through overhanging greenery with power lines in the trees above to join a road. You are now in Hambledon on the Greensand Way (GW).

3. Turn right to pass in front of a house (Matteryes) and then turn into the driveway of the house and immediately go left up some steps (fingerpost GW). Go uphill to a kissing gate then follow the grassy footpath round to the right. Keep straight ahead to another kissing gate. Follow the path across the field and up the slope, go through the

kissing gate and turn right onto a lane with Hambledon church on your left. At the end of the lane, bear right on a bridleway and continue between fields. It is worth pausing at intervals to look over your left shoulder at the extensive views towards the North Downs. At the T- junction turn right along a lane. Ignore the bridleway as it turns left up the bank and keep on the lane. Just past a large house below you on the right, turn left up the bank and then right along the bridleway to continue ahead. Soon you will have extensive views of the South Downs, Black Down and Hindhead. The views are lost when the path goes between trees and skirts a barely glimpsed house and gardens. Take the next footpath signed to the right, now leaving the Greensand Way. The path, narrow and slightly overgrown, takes you downhill through shrubbery to a metalled drive. Turn left to follow the drive through gardens to the entrance gates and a lane (Markwick Lane).

4. Turn right along the lane taking care to watch for traffic. After 400m/$^{1}/_{4}$mile you come to footpaths signed to left and right. Take the footpath to the right through a metal gate beside a brick wall, with a small pond on your right. As the wall on your left ends, follow the wider farm track downhill, again enjoying good views to the south. At the T-junction, turn left along a broad bridleway. Soon there is woodland on the right. Just before the trees end take the footpath signed to the right and follow this path through the woods to emerge by going over a stile. Turn left along the edge of the field. Go through one kissing gate and proceed ahead to another. After the second gate cross the field diagonally right to go over a stile and reach a lane.

5. Turn right along the lane (Hookhouse Road), to go past the converted barn on the left. Then, as the lane goes off to the right, keep close to the fence to go straight ahead into a field through a large gate. The footpath across this field is indistinct; make your way diagonally right in the direction of a metal gate. Just before reaching this gate, turn right to go along the field edge making for a stile visible ahead. Once over the stile, bear left down into a dip and across to another stile leading into trees. Go straight through this small patch of woodland, passing a pond on your left and ignoring a footpath to the right, to emerge at another stile. Bear left across the field to the opposite corner, go through a gate and proceed along a fenced track with playing fields on your left. At the T-junction, turn left along the bridleway and go over a stile to emerge at the northern end of Dunsfold Common. Turn right in front of the cottages, with a pond to your left and continue ahead with a hedge on your right. Cross over a driveway and keep straight on. The path comes close to the road at one point but you can soon go to the right again to walk along in front of the houses on your right. Shortly after the Post Office you reach the Sun Inn.

6. Immediately after the Sun Inn turn right into Oak Tree Lane, passing the oak tree on your left. Keep on the path between a cottage and a pond to join Mill Lane. Continue past the bungalows and then the road becomes a path (bridleway) descending through trees. Carry on to a junction of bridleways where you turn right over the metalled bridge and then immediately left along a footpath. This path goes across another bridge and through a gate then continues alongside the water. After a stile you can divert left to look at the Holy Well before following the footpath up to Dunsfold Church.

7. Pass in front of the church gate and over the grass keeping close to the hedge. Take the bridleway to the left. Pass old farm buildings on your right and, as the farm track goes sharply right, go ahead to cross a small field. Bear slightly to the right on a signed footpath to a stile, go over this, continue along the field edge with the fence to your left and turn right at the corner. Leave the field by a stile and turn left along a metalled track to enjoy lovely views of the hills around Hascombe. Just after a pond on your right, turn left before the gated entrance to Field Place and very soon go over a stile on the right. Follow the direction of the fingerpost and go straight over the grass and then down the steep incline to the stile visible ahead. Cross this and turn right on the track to keep ahead through the gate to Dunsley Farm. Go ahead at a junction, with the farm house to your left, and then walk to the right along a bridleway between trees. Keep forward as you join the main track, and when the bridleway turns to the right, go straight on along the footpath bearing left. Having entered a field over a narrow wooden footbridge, go straight across towards woods and turn left at the far field edge onto a bridleway. As the footpath continues into woods, walk straight ahead. When you meet a driveway go ahead between two barns and through a gate into a field. Go across the field to a lane, bearing slightly right to find the stile.

8. Go left along the lane (Vann Lane) and very soon take the footpath on the right. Follow this path over two awkward little stiles and then another stile into a long narrow field. Make for a stile at the far end then go ahead to pass farm buildings on your left and stables on your right. At a crossing of paths, go left through a gate into a field (there is a stile hidden behind the large tree beside the gate). Continue ahead with the field boundary on your left and cross a stile next to an old cottage. Go along the drive to reach a lane, passing a sign to Yew Tree Cottage on your left. Turn left to walk along the road until it bends left, just past the drive to a house, Rystead. Take the footpath on the right, following the direction of the fingerpost. Go left just before a gate and then turn right at a T-junction to emerge from the trees into a field. Continue up the slope with the hedge on your left. Ignore the first gap in the hedge and enjoy the views of Hascombe Hill and Hydon's Ball to your right. As the views disappear behind trees, go through a gap in the hedge to continue in the same direction, with the hedge now on your right and views of Black Down on your left. Continue ahead passing into a second field (waymarked footpath) and keeping trees and the hedge still on your right. At the far corner of the field where there are crossing paths, turn left along the footpath along the field boundary, still with trees on your right. As the field edge dips to the right, keep straight ahead across the field and on through a metal gate. Follow the track between houses down to a lane and turn right.

You will soon pass Chiddingfold Post Office on your right. At the T-junction, cross carefully over the road to reach the Green.

If you started from Witley station, now follow sections 1 and 2 to return to the point where you joined. Here turn left and follow the Greensand Way back to the station.

From Witley station, turn left out of the brick station buildings and walk past the car park to the end of the road. Cross over bearing slightly right to turn left onto the footpath (fingerpost) going between houses. This path emerges onto a busy road (A283) at a fingerpost with Greensand Way (GW) markers; you will follow this well marked long distance path until you meet the route. Turn left, and almost immediately cross very carefully over the road at the next fingerpost to go along the minor road ahead, Wormley Lane. Continue down the road until it turns right at the entrance to Hambledon Park. Turn left here onto a gravelled bridleway uphill and continue until you emerge onto open heathland with Manor Cottage ahead of you. Take the bridleway in front of the cottage, passing the garage of the cottage on your left and go uphill to emerge in an open area. Follow the Greensand Way as it goes left – from here you have wonderful views of Black Down and the South Downs. Continue on the footpath downhill through light woodland until it reaches the road (Malthouse Lane) at the entrance to St, Dominic's School, where you turn left. You are now in Hambledon village, an ancient settlement mentioned in the Domesday Book. Continue to walk carefully (there is no pavement) along the road, passing the right turning to Woodlands Road, until you reach a house on your right called Matteryes where you turn into the driveway. Now follow the directions from section 3 to complete the walk. Return to the station via the same route.

Note. Walks 11 and 13 both explore the areas around Dunsfold and Vann Lane. They meet/overlap at sections 11: 2, 10, 4, 8 and 13: 4, 7, 8, 3. See sketch maps.

14 Chalk streams and rolling downs in rural Hampshire – New Alresford, Ovington, Tichborne and Cheriton

Bryce and Edwina's walk

Length: 18km/11¼miles (sections 1-4, 6-10) with a shorter version of 12km/7½miles (sections 1-5).

Maps: OS Landranger 185; Explorer 132.

Start: GR 588325 Alresford station car park (Mid Hants Railway, popularly known as the Watercress Line).
From the A31 Alton/Winchester road, take the B3047 to New Alresford and follow the signs to the Mid Hants railway station.

Transport: Alresford is served by buses from Winchester and Peterfield.

Refreshments: Alresford station buffet; the Bush PH Ovington; the Tichborne Arms, Tichborne; selection of pubs, restaurants and cafés in New Alresford.

Introduction: This walk, which uses the Wayfarers Walk and the Itchen Way takes you along the beautiful chalk streams and peaceful rolling farmland of Hampshire and there are beautiful views from all the high ground. Rural England at its best!

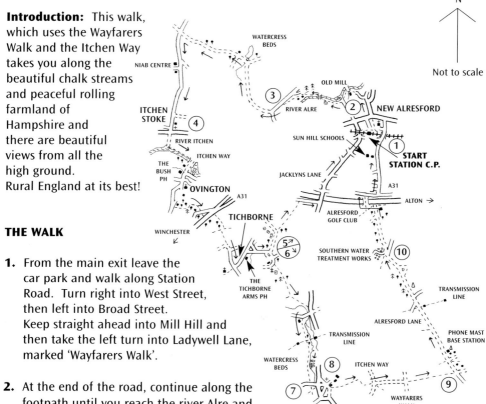

THE WALK

1. From the main exit leave the car park and walk along Station Road. Turn right into West Street, then left into Broad Street. Keep straight ahead into Mill Hill and then take the left turn into Ladywell Lane, marked 'Wayfarers Walk'.

2. At the end of the road, continue along the footpath until you reach the river Alre and follow this path as it bears left along the river and passes the Old Fulling Mill. Where the river flows right, turn right to walk parallel to it and take the path along the end of the cottages. The Walk passes the Recreation Ground and then re-joins the river. Cross the river beside the brick building, continue for about 20m/22yards and cross a tributary over a small bridge. Continue to a road and follow the public footpath, still the Wayfarers Walk, parallel to the power line poles until you reach another road.

3. Turn left, cross the road and continue along the Wayfarers Walk. Go forward for about 800m/¹/₂mile turning left when you reach the vehicle height restriction bar. Cross the streams with a view of the watercress beds on your right and continue past the cottage on your right. Go forward about 800m/¹/₂mile to a road. Turn left, leaving the Wayfarers Walk, and go up the road, passing the NIAB centre on your right, to Itchen Stoke. The road walking is more than compensated by the fine views all around. The chapel on your left at the crossroads is well worth a visit.

4. Cross the road and take the path signposted 'Ovington $\frac{1}{2}$ mile' to reach the river Itchen. Turn left on the Itchen Way and enjoy this beautiful, peaceful stretch of the river. Cross the road on the Itchen Way and go uphill past St Peter's Church to Ovington House. Keeping the wall on your left, follow the direction of the fingerpost in the hedge on your left hand side just past the Lodge Gate. Go left following around the field boundary to the top of the hill. Do not turn right but look for the narrow, overgrown path which leads ahead to a large layby on the A31. Go left and cross the A31, taking great care as this is a busy road, take the Itchen Way path immediately opposite and follow it along the right side of the field. At the field end, go right and then immediately left (no fingerposts at this point), go down the field ahead and continue on the path towards Tichborne. The church should be visible in the trees ahead. Enter the village and turn left to the Tichborne Arms. Shortly after the pub, bear right following the sign towards the Pottery; this lane is marked 'Tichborne House, No Right of Way'. Cross over the stream, pass the pottery on your right and stop at the T-junction.

5. For the shorter walk, turn left, then at the fork keep right up the slope. Take the field path slightly to your right which goes diagonally across the field to reach the A31. Go right and right again on to the path along the A31 to a road bridge. Turn left over the bridge and walk up Jacklyns Lane into New Alresford. Immediately after going under the railway bridge, turn right to reach the car park where you use the side entrance.

6. For the longer walk, turn right and cross the stile by the brick pillars of Tichborne House into a field and walk along the right hand field boundary. Cross two stiles and go forward across the next field to a stile. Bear left across the field to the road. Turn right and right again – signposted 'Tichborne'. Cross the streams and just after the bridge by a willow tree turn left, signposted 'Itchen Way/Wayfarers Walk'. Go through the gate and past the cottage on your right. Cross a stile and keep to the left field boundary with the stream on your left. Go forward crossing two stiles and three fields to reach a minor road in Cheriton. Turn left to reach the main road.

7. At the main road, turn right. After the telephone box, walk to the end of the green and turn left to the post office. After a short distance, turn right with the 'Freemans Yard' sign ahead. Cross the bridge over the stream and turn right past the school and take the footpath on the left by Martyr Well House, signposted 'Wayfarers Walk'.

8. Climb uphill between fences to open ground with a beautiful view ahead. Cross a stile into the field and go right uphill following the field boundary to a stile leading onto a green lane. Keep ahead between hedges on the Wayfarers Walk. At the second crossing track, the Wayfarers Walk turns right to Hinton Ampner. Do not turn right but continue ahead to the field end.

9. Turn left onto Alresford Lane (no sign). Continue on this path, passing a mobile phone base station and mast on your right, for 1¼km/¾mile until you meet another road coming in from your left. Carry straight on for a short distance; ignore the road going off to your right and go on uphill bearing left to walk on a path signposted 'Right of Way'. Continue uphill passing another phone mast to the fork, where you bear left and continue to the Southern Water treatment works, ignoring all side turnings and paths.

10. Take the waymarked bridleway path in front of you and go ahead ignoring all side paths to reach the golf course. Go past the 7th tee, carefully cross the fairways and pass a stone building on your right to reach the A31. Turn left, to walk beside the main road for a short distance, then turn right to cross the road bridge and go right to a road which you follow around to the left and then up the hill. You are now on the Wayfarers Walk once again and will pass Sun Hill Schools on your left. Cross the railway bridge (the station is to your left) and take the footpath left along the railway. Turn right with the cemetery on your left and after a row of cottages, turn left and cross the cemetery to reach Station Road. Turn left and return to the car park by the main entrance.

15 Peaceful Paths in the Low Weald – Ebernoe to Northchapel

Hazel's walk

Length:
12½km/8miles.

Maps:
OS Landranger
186; Explorer 133.

Start:
GR 976278 Ebernoe Church car park.
From the A283 going south from Northchapel, take the first turning on the left (Streels Lane) signposted Ebernoe and Balls Cross. Continue along this road for about 2¼km/1½miles, through a cricket ground with the pavilion on your left. Then, a short distance past a red telephone box, also on the left, turn right at a concealed turning, signposted Ebernoe Church (Holy Trinity Church) and School House. This leads to a parking area beside the church.

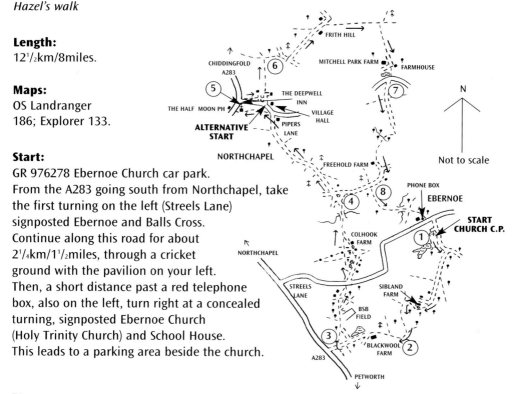

74

Alternative start: GR 952295 Northchapel at the junction of A283 and Pipers Lane. Roadside parking in Pipers Lane. Start at section 5.

Transport: There is no public transport to Ebernoe but buses from Haslemere, Midhurst and Chichester pass through Northchapel.

Refreshments: the Half Moon PH or the Deepwell Inn, Northchapel.

Introduction: Ebernoe lies in ancient woodland and is one of the most peaceful places there is. This quiet Sussex hamlet is renowned for two things - the cricket pitch through which the road runs (boundary fielding can have its own excitements!) and the annual Horn Fair, held on 25 July. As well as a traditional fair, the main event of the day is a cricket match and a whole sheep roast (in earlier times complete with horns). At 1pm the vicar and the cricketers process to the pavilion to eat; later the "horns" - now a mounted trophy - are presented to the highest scoring batsman on the winning side. The spring flowers make this walk very special for me. The walk is in two halves, wooded at first, then into fields with open views. There are a few stiles and hardly any hills but it can be muddy in winter.

THE WALK

1. Stand facing the church in the car park and go to the right hand side to follow a path down beside the churchyard wall, passing a gate to the church entrance (do go in and look at the church if you have time). Continue forward and go down steps to a pond on the right. Near the far side of the pond, take a path to the left taking you down steps and go over a small bridge. Carry on till you reach a T-junction, where you turn right and continue uphill until you come to a gate with a cattle grid. Go through the gate, and then follow the broad track round to the right by a fingerpost. Continue forward on the broad track until you come to some buildings and a house (Sibland Farm - no name) on the right hand side. Walk on for 100m/110yards to a gate directly in front of you with a fingerpost on the left. Go through the gate and continue forward on the path which meanders through a beech wood and across a bridge over a ditch by a large beech tree. Continue through a holly and beech copse with fallen trunks of trees on the side until another footbridge comes into view. Cross over the bridge and continue on to a breach in a large bank ahead, where you turn left by a fingerpost. Continue with the bank on your right hand side. Where the bank turns to the right, keep beside it a short way and reach another fingerpost. Take the path bearing left, on level ground, away from the bank. This path meanders through light woodland - in the spring this area has wild daffodils on both sides of the path – and cross a wooden bridge. After several hundred metres/yards, walk between two parts of a fallen beech tree that has been cut to allow the path to pass through. Turn right at the next fingerpost. After a short while the path bears left by a bank and a field on the right, up to a T-junction with a fingerpost.

2. Turn right and with the field over to your right follow the footpath signs, going slightly downhill. Continue forward past another fingerpost with a field on the left. The path starts to rise gently to farm buildings with lakes on the right hand side (Blackwool Farm). Walk forward on a made up road, keeping the lakes on the right hand side and ignoring a fairly wide track on the right at the end of the lake.

3. Near the top of the slight rise, turn right opposite a fingerpost (bridleway) towards the British School of Ballooning (BSB) launch site and Caravan Club (CC) site. Take the left path at the bridleway fingerpost, also signposted to BSB launch site. At the BSB launch site field take the rutted bridleway to the left of the field entrance, keeping the field on your right and carry on along this rutted track to a fingerpost in woodland. Branch right and keep forward past further fingerposts, passing cottages seen through the trees to your left and reach a road. Cross over the road to Colhook Farm, where there are benches and a small pond and take the farm track/road to the right of the roadside bench, keeping the pond and cottages on your right. Turn left immediately before the second telegraph pole (opposite a small lime green conifer in a cottage garden). Continue, keeping to the right of the open area and go ahead into woodland on the main track, ignoring the small path on the left. On reaching a crossing track with a fingerpost, keep straight ahead on the bridleway. Continue forward on this bridleway over two more crossing tracks, ignoring the paths on your right by a bridleway fingerpost. Eventually you will walk through a (quite often) very boggy area. Continue on over a stream with a delightful little bridge (when viewed from the right hand stream side) going up a slight incline, soon reaching a small plantation on the left, with a barbed wire fence. Pass a fingerpost on the left, (Public Bridleway), still continuing in the same direction.

4. Cross a metalled road and continue on the bridleway opposite. Go straight over two crossing tracks, and continue forward, ignoring paths to right and left. Go ahead on a public bridleway following the direction of the fingerpost, ignoring the path going off to the left into a field. Pass a fingerpost on the left, ignoring the footpath to the right and when you come to a junction with a fingerpost on the right, continue straight up the farm road with farm machinery on the left. Shortly afterwards you will pass a farm on the right. When you reach the road, continue past a small building on the left to a stile and fingerpost. Go over the stile and take the footpath across the field following the direction of the fingerpost towards the right-hand edge of the field. Go through a gap in the hedge and continue on with buildings on your right and the church straight ahead. Keep close to the hedge and cross a stile in the right hand corner of the field. Continue ahead to a kissing gate into the churchyard and go through the churchyard with the church on the right (St Michael and All Angels, Northchapel). Carry on, passing a house on the left (Thornfalcon House), until you come to the A283, with the Half Moon pub opposite. Turn right and continue up the road to the Deepwell Inn.

5. Immediately after the Inn, turn right into Pipers Lane, and walk across the common towards the children's play area. Continue between the hedge on your left and the play area on your right until you reach a metalled road just before the village hall.

Turn left onto the metalled road towards the cottages on your right and carry on past these cottages into a field. Walk up this field keeping the hedge on the left and at the top, go through a gap in the hedge, into another field. Continue ahead keeping the hedge on the left – there are lovely views of the countryside behind you. Go through a gate into a wood called The Frith, which is very good for bluebells and foxgloves. Bear right to a fingerpost (Public Bridleway) ahead, having ignored the downhill path and continue forward, ignoring a path to the right and one to the left.

6. At the junction of bridleways (fingerposted) keep right towards a metal gate. Go through the gate and turn left onto a metalled road. Further up the road, you will come to buildings on the right hand side, a large house (Frith Hill), stables and out-buildings. The road then becomes a gravel path. Continue on this path past the house on the right, ignoring a footpath on the left, and then look out for a public bridleway fingerpost, shortly before a cottage, pointing to the right onto a path between holly bushes. Follow this path, soon to go through a gate onto a grassy path. On the left is a very attractive cottage, and on the right are beautiful views of the South Downs. Continue forwards and go through another gate, onto a path between holly bushes and follow this gradually downhill for just under 800m/$^1/_2$mile. When you reach a gate on the right hand side, with a fingerpost (Public Footpath), turn right through the gate into a field, following the line of telegraph poles across the field. Go through a gap in the hedge to the next field, still following the telegraph poles, and then on to a cart track slightly downhill. You will pass farm buildings on the right and left, then a farm house (Mitchell Park Farm) on your left. Almost immediately, follow the direction of the fingerpost onto the grass, continuing downhill under telegraph wires, until you reach a pond. Carry on with the pond on your right until you reach a stile in front of you. Go over the stile, up the steps, straight ahead to a road (which is a continuation of Pipers Lane).

7. Cross the road to a public footpath fingerpost by a gate. Go along this path, keeping to the right hand edge of the field, until you reach a crossing path in the next field. Continue straight on, following the fingerpost (Public Footpath), ignoring the right and left paths. Go into the next field and at the end of the path turn right by a fingerpost and carry on along the left hand side of the field with Black Down ahead. Continue a short distance straight on until you reach a fingerpost pointing to the left with a stile. Go over the stile into a field, turn immediately right and continue down a grassy cart track, with trees either side, for a short distance until you get to another field. Walk diagonally left across the field, in the direction indicated by the fingerpost, towards the hedge on the far side. Bear right at the top of the rise, keeping the hedge on your left until you reach a stile and gate on your left with a fingerpost. Turn left with a farm (Freehold Farm – no sign) straight ahead and continue forward to another gate and stile with farm buildings on your right. Cross this stile and continue forward, keeping these buildings on the right. Carry on ahead onto a tarmac road, with a fingerpost on your left, passing more farm buildings further along on the left. Continue to walk on the tarmac road, downhill, until you reach a fingerpost and stile on the right.

8. Turn left opposite this stile, leaving the tarmac road and keeping the woods on your right. Keep ahead until you reach a stile into another field. Cross the stile and continue up a small incline in the field, keeping woods on your right and look for a fingerpost in the holly hedge (which is often overgrown). Then turn sharply left, following the direction of the fingerpost across the field to a stile and fingerpost into the woods. Go over the stile, down a sharp descent and across a bridge over a small stream. Carry on forward up a narrow path with bracken each side in summer, passing a fingerpost half-way up the hill on your right, to a fingerpost at the top on your left. Go straight ahead, ignoring the right hand path. Continue forward, coming to a further area with high bracken in summer. At the fingerpost bear right, ignoring the path on the left, to go on past another fingerpost with a large house and buildings (Ebernoe House) on the right. Ahead is a gate, leading onto the Ebernoe Road. Turn left, walk a short distance and turn right into the drive that leads to Ebernoe Church and School House. Continue up the drive bearing right until you reach the car park.

16 Across the Hampshire Hangers from Petersfield to Liss

Kate N's walk

Length: 16km/10miles.

Maps: OS Landranger 197; Explorer 133.

Start: GR 743236 Petersfield railway station. This is a linear walk from one station to the other with an easy return to the start by train. By car, follow the signs to the station from the A3 or A272 and park at Petersfield station. An alternative is to park in Liss and take the train to Petersfield. Liss is signed from the A3. From the south, follow the main road round for about 1¼km/¾mile until you reach a T-junction. Turn left, go ahead and after passing shops on the left, turn left to the station. There are car parks near the station on either side of the level crossing.

Transport: Both Petersfield and Liss stations are on the London Waterloo/Portsmouth line. Buses run between Liss and Petersfield.

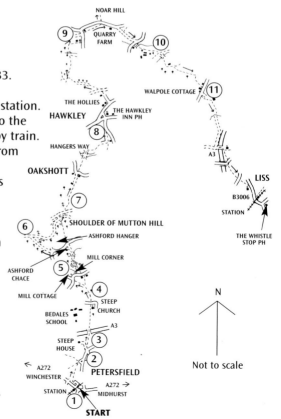

Refreshments: the Whistle Stop PH, Liss; the Hawkley Inn, Hawkley; selection of cafés, pubs and restaurants in Petersfield.

Introduction: I like to leave my car at home when I walk and to go from one place to another rather than in a circle; this route allows me to do both. It follows the Hangers Way (marked by round stickers with a green arrow and a tree inside it) as far as Hawkley and is well marked with fingerposts. It can be muddy in places and there is one steep climb up Ashford Hanger, which can be very slippery when wet. This is lovely countryside and the open views along the way are an excellent reward for all the effort. (Hangers are the richest woodland on English chalk – a series of steep sided wooded hills.)

THE WALK

1. On leaving the station, turn left over the level crossing. Cross the road and continue forward to the garage, then turn right at the Hangers Way fingerpost and continue along the path behind houses. On reaching a four way crossing, follow the path ahead and go downhill to reach the road.

2. Turn left (Hangers Way sticker affixed to a lamp post opposite), cross to the pavement and continue up the road to the bend, re-cross the road and with Steep House to your left continue up the Hangers Way footpath.

3. Cross the A3 by the footbridge and go forward, bearing right along the path and passing the grounds of Bedales School on the left. Ignore any turnings to the right. On reaching the road with Steep church on the right, turn right and then almost immediately left to cross into a small grassy recreation area.

4. Bear left ahead to follow a well walked path down through the woods. This path is often very muddy but there is a narrow path off to the left as an alternative. Go over a stile – with views of Shoulder of Mutton Hill ahead - and continue left along the edge of the field to a kissing gate onto the road. Turn right and head down the road to pass Mill Cottage on your left. The Hangers Way continues along the road but it is better to take the footpath indicated by a fingerpost on your left before the bend, and go uphill on a narrow fenced path beside the garage of Mill Corner. This path passes a small waterfall on your left, goes over the stream and then up four steps. Turn left here to rejoin the Hangers Way (coming from the right).

5. Follow the well made path with a fenced area (Little Langleys Conservation Area) on the right, and several ponds to right and left amongst the trees, before crossing a stile and in a short distance a small wooden bridge. Then bear right onto a gravel drive to reach a road at which you turn left, passing a house called Ashford Chace. At the sharp left hand bend, turn right following the Hangers Way along a path which broadens into a wider track as it climbs Ashford Hill. Pass the large Ashford Hanger sign as you start to climb and ignoring the track on the right, continue uphill and follow the Hangers Way sign as the track takes a sharp right hand bend.

6. As the chalky track goes uphill, views of the South Downs open out on the right. Continue on, ignoring the path with a stile on the right. On reaching the top of the hill, spare a moment to take in the view south from the top of the Shoulder of Mutton Hill. Then with your back to the notice board, walk forward through a gap in the fence and continue forward to a field boundary. Turn right and walk briefly on the level gravel track, then turn left at the stile and go downhill through the beech woods continuing through a gate and over two stiles to reach a steep field with a lovely view. In spring this field is covered in cowslips.

7. Go downhill, cross the stile at the bottom into a field and over another stile by a house leading into a tarmac driveway. Turn right and continue down the gravel track to the road with Middle Oakshott House on your left. Turn right and then left over a stile into a field and follow this grassy and somewhat uneven up and down path until it divides. Here take the left hand fork down the slope to cross a stile and then the stream by a bridge. Continue forward on a well defined but somewhat overgrown path through a field. As the path goes uphill much later, it passes a house with a swimming pool and a Hangers Way fingerpost on the right continuing uphill until it meets a road. Keep forward along this into Hawkley. At the crossroads, where the church, village green and seats are in front of you, continue ahead. If you want to stop for refreshment, turn right for the Hawkley Inn, a short way up on the left and return to the green to continue the walk.

8. Leave the Hangers Way for a while and walk on with the lych gate of the church on your right and then a little later, Hawkley House on the left. Continue along the road and turn left at the fingerpost down a narrow lane by a house called The Hollies. Cross a stile into a fenced path having passed houses on the way. Cross another stile over a track and go over a further stile into a field and follow the direction of the fingerpost diagonally left across this field. At the corner, go through the gateway and turn left, to go straight ahead on a path between two hedges to emerge at a field edge. From here, follow the direction of the waymarker on the post ahead of you and bear slightly right across the corner of the field toward the trees ahead to a footpath into the woods, which then goes up a slope. Turn right to rejoin the Hangers Way. Ignore the path to the right and go down and then up steps and very shortly over a stile into a field. Go round the edge of this field, cross a further stile into another field and walk by the hedge, then cross a stile to come out onto a road.

9. Turn left, pass a pond and Vann House on the left and go uphill ignoring a path on the left at the brow of the hill. Then turn right over a stile beside the Hangers Way sign to go forward across two fields. Go over two further stiles to emerge onto a minor road. Turn right and walk through a small ford having passed a Hangers Way sign on your left. Here you leave the Hangers Way for the last time. Continue ahead along the road and shortly after passing Quarry Farm join a byway (fingerpost) on your right that takes you downhill to join another road where you turn right.

After a short distance (before you reach a house) go left over a stile at a fingerpost (Footpath) and continue over another stile and a little bridge. In the garden on the right are three beehives. Follow the path over a stile going left uphill and over four more stiles and through a kissing gate to reach a large field.

10. Go straight ahead downhill over a small bridge and uphill at the edge of a field with woods on the right. Turn left at the fingerpost to go towards the building in the middle of the field. Pass this and keeping below the fence and the wood ahead go to a stile on the far edge of the wood. Continue in the same direction over the fields following waymarks and fingerposts to a wooden farm gate in the right hand corner of the field near the houses, continue over a stile in the garden fence into an orchard and follow the waymarks and stiles through the garden to the road.

11. Turn right and after passing Walpole Cottage on your right, turn left down a wide track and take the footpath beside the farm entrance into a fenced field. Go through the gate and past the farm on your left. Bear right to walk along the hedgeline and then go on through three fields passing a barn and crossing a stream eventually to walk parallel to and above the A3. When you reach a crossing path leading to a bridge over the A3, turn left and follow the right hand path diagonally across the field to a stile. Go over this, turn right into a narrow path and follow this till you reach a road. Cross the road and, taking the path with houses on your left, carry on until you reach another road. Cross this and go into the churchyard and head towards the gates on your left. Go through the gates and at the road, turn right and go downhill to reach Liss station.

17 A hidden corner of Sussex - Stedham, Iping, Chithurst, Milland and Titty Hill

Joyce's walk

Length: 16km/10miles (sections 1-8) with an extension of $^3/_4$km/$^1/_2$mile to Milland at section 6) or a shorter version of 10km/6miles (sections 1, 9, 10, 7 and 8).

Maps: OS Landranger 197; Explorer 133.

Start: GR 862224 Stedham Village Green, roadside parking just past the telephone box on the left.
Follow the A272 from Midhurst towards Petersfield. Take the second turning on the right, signposted to Stedham, and park on the road close to the village green.

Transport: A number of bus routes go along the A272 between Midhurst and Petersfield and some go into Stedham village.

Refreshments: the Rising Sun PH at Milland; the Hamilton Arms, School Lane, Stedham (not on route but close to start); selection of pubs, teashops and restaurants in Midhurst 3km/1$^3/_4$miles away.

Introduction: This route shows West Sussex at its best, with good distant views, varied terrain, lovely wild flowers and butterflies in season, colourful gardens and crop fields, pretty villages and interesting churches (all well worth visiting) as well as the serpentine river Rother. Few walks in Sussex are free of mud after heavy rain or without a large number of stiles, and this is no exception!

THE WALK

Long walk 16km/10miles

1. With your back to the village green and the phone box to your left on the opposite side of the road, turn right and walk along the road passing the turning right to the church.
Just before you reach the bridge over the river Rother ahead, turn left onto a bridleway; the river is now on your right. Continue beside the river until it loops away to the right where you should remain on the path going straight ahead until you come to a five-bar iron gate across the path. Turn left onto tarmac, bear slightly right and then left to go down a cobbled path (waymarker – Bridleway) beside an entrance to a large house. Be careful as the cobbles can be slippery. At the road, turn right and cross the bridge. This is Iping. A footpath fingerpost points the way into the church grounds. Follow the footpath through the churchyard and round a large lime tree to a stile and into a field. Cross the field diagonally to your left, heading for a large half dead tree, to a wooden four-bar gate and stile. Cross the stile and continue ahead with the hedge to your left and then follow the field edge round to the right until you come to a post pointing left to a bridge with chains across. Cross the bridge and go into the field (there may be an electric fence here, so take care in opening it). Head slightly left across here to a hedge with a stile and then keeping farm buildings to your right, continue to a stile. Carry on along the farm track to the left until you reach the road and then turn right. This is Chithurst. **To continue the short walk, go to section 9.**

2. By the church, turn left into the large driveway which has a footpath fingerpost. Continue along the driveway through a gateway into a parking area, then bear left, as indicated by yellow waymarks, to walk over grass with the stone wall and later a yew hedge of Chithurst Manor Gardens on your left. In the corner, cross a stile and keep straight ahead through a rough field to the opposite hedge, go over a stile and turn right. At the top of the rise and before reaching the power lines, look for a footpath arrow on a waymarker post on your right close to a stile with a steep drop. Go over this through the hedge and follow the path bearing left to reach and cross two small stiles close together onto Brier Lane (unsigned), a restricted by-way, marked by a post with a red/purple arrow.

3. Turn right and in 100m/110yards, turn left over a stile to head towards and beyond an electricity pylon, keeping the fence on your right. Go over another stile beside a metal gate and a third which takes you down onto a minor road. Turn left and continue along the road passing Malt House on your right. At the top of the hill turn left at a fingerpost onto another restricted byway (Green Lane – unsigned), close to the drive to Holmhill and Holmlea. Continue along this byway for 1km/²/₃mile to reach a tarmac road.

4. Turn right towards Borden Wood and Milland and go down the hill until the road swings right. Walk straight ahead and follow a fingerpost at the side of a wooden five-bar gate. Continue along the track with sweet chestnut coppice on the left. Further along on the right is a green metal seven-bar gate and a fingerpost indicating the bridleway which is the smaller track to the right. Follow this track which can be very muddy and waterlogged in winter. When the track improves, the field to the left can be very colourful when planted with oil seed rape, and the banks have wild daffodils in spring. At the next road, Cook's Pond Road, turn left and continue past Bobbolds Farm on your right, then a cottage, Kingsmead, on the left.

5. Shortly after this take the next track to the right signed to Pinchers, where the fingerpost is hidden round the corner. Cross a stile beside an iron gate and keeping the hedge to your right, continue to a fingerpost at a corner where you turn left across the field to reach the left hand of two metal gates. Cross a railway sleeper bridge, go through another gate and bear diagonally right across the field as indicated by the fingerpost aiming for a gap in the trees where a metal gate will become visible. Go over a footbridge and through this gate to cross a field to another gate and stile in the far left corner. Now walk ahead towards a large clump of trees and pass between them and the fence to a fingerpost where you turn right, into a farmyard with a large iron gate and a stile. Continue through the farmyard (Waldergrove Farm – no sign) and through an opening beside an automatic gate onto a drive leading to the road.

6. *If you wish to visit Milland, turn left to walk up the road and the Rising Sun Pub is on the right at the crossroads. There is also a large green opposite for a picnic. To return to the route, at the crossroads by the pub turn right along the road towards Fernhurst, using the pavement. Just after the 40mph speed limit and a 'beware of ducks' sign, go over the road to a fingerpost and stile. Cross a field diagonally to another stile in the far right corner. Continue ahead keeping the hedge to your right, cross another stile, a bridge and a track to another stile into a field. Follow the fingerpost direction across the field to a stile just to the right of the house to your left to rejoin the main route at [A].*

Turn left on the road and then right into the next entrance (Myers) which has a fingerpost in the hedge. Turn immediately right over a stile and follow the path to another stile to the right of the house on the far side of the field. **[A]** Cross this stile, a railway sleeper bridge, and a second stile into a field where a waymarked stile can be seen on the far side. Cross the field and this stile which leads to a stone bridge and a second stile, into a small field with a dead tree in the centre. Continue to a further stile and plank bridge leading to larger field with good views to Titty Hill to your right. Go ahead over this field to another stile and cross this. Now walk along the left hand edge of this field to the next stile beside a gate and fingerpost and cross the grassy track to another stile. Go over this and bear right up the field towards a stile in front of the barn in the distance. Cross this stile, through a gap in the fence to a fingerpost and keep bearing left across yet another stile to reach a shingle track. At the shingle track turn left, then immediately right onto a grassy footpath around Alfords Farm (no sign) to a stile and gate, then turn left onto a tarmac drive, and quickly right over a stile and follow the edge of the field parallel to the drive. Turn right at the corner of the field and continue to a fingerpost by a stile which you cross out onto a tarmac lane (Lambourne Lane) where you turn right. Continue along the lane until the main track turns left. Carry on straight ahead on a rougher track, which can be very muddy, signed as a public right of way with a green waymarker. In spring there are wild daffodils to the left and in summer there are many butterflies here. Continue on this broad track for just under $1^1/_4$km/$^3/_4$mile and at the top of the long slope there are houses on the right. This is Titty Hill. At the junction of wide tracks, bear to the left and take the next turning right, signposted bridleway. Continue up the fairly steep slope past an old farmhouse on the right and go through a metal gate with a fingerpost, keeping to the hedge on your left.

7. Go through another gate and continue down the track, ignoring a fingerpost pointing left, until the track joins the driveway to a large house called Tentworth (no sign). At the second fingerpost on the left opposite an entrance signed The Lodge, bear left over the open grassy area to pick up a track in the corner (fingerpost on your right). Keep going gently downhill, over crossing paths and you will see a gate ahead. Passing a bridleway marker post, continue downhill on a sunken narrow track between high banks. Near the bottom, swing left and descend onto a wide track. Turn right at the bottom to emerge near a cottage on the left.

8. In front of the cottage as the main track bears right, turn left up a very narrow and steep path. Turn right on a broad track until a footpath waymarker points left and up a slope; take this path until it reaches a road. At the road, turn left and at Woodgate Farm turn right and go up the grassy slope. Follow the field edge keeping the fence to your right, until it bears slightly left where you will find a marker post next to a telephone pole indicating a stile and a footpath to the right. Cross this stile and walk down the field, keeping the hedge to your right, to another stile in the corner of the field which leads down to a road, Stedham Lane.

Turn right and then almost immediately left onto a footpath on a downwards slope to a stile and continue straight ahead which brings you out opposite Stedham Mill with its attractive gardens. Cross the weir and follow the lane which eventually goes round to the right, following the churchyard boundary. Turn left at the road junction to go back to the start.

Short walk 10km/6miles

9. Follow the directions in section 1. In Chithurst, after passing Chithurst church on your left, keep ahead on the narrow road as it goes uphill. Continue along the road, passing the Chithurst Buddhist monastery on your left, round a bend to the right. At the T-junction, take the left fork and follow the lane until it turns left where you take the bridleway ahead of you and follow it downhill (bearing left at the start) into woodland. Continue to walk along this clearly defined bridleway through light woodland going over a bridge and then uphill onto more level ground until it passes an old stone house on the left with gardens leading down to a stream and Moor Cottage on your right. Ignoring the paths off to your right and left, continue along what is now a wider earth/gravel track until it reaches a road emerging opposite Robins Farm.

10. Turn right along the road and almost immediately left up a track (fingerpost Public Right of Way) between houses. Follow this old tarmac track as it goes uphill passing houses on the right and then into woodland. At the cattle grid, take the right fork continuing uphill on a sandy/stony track until, as the path levels out, you reach a metal gate. Go through the gate into an open area and continue on the sandy drive for a short distance until you reach a farmhouse ahead of you. Turn left here and continue straight on, ignoring a signed path to the left, until you reach a black painted house and outbuildings on your right. Cross over the stile in the corner of a field and then almost immediately go over another one beside a gate on your right. Keeping the hedge on your left walk along the field boundary until you reach a metal gate in the left hand corner of the field and a crossing track (fingerpost Public Bridleway). Do not go through the gate but turn right here and walk ahead keeping the hedge on your left. **To complete the walk follow the directions in sections 7 and 8.**

18 Into the unknown! Petworth, No Man's Land, Wilderness and Limbo

Richard's walk

Length: 16½km/10¼ miles (sections 1, 2, 4-7). This walk can be shortened by 1km/⅔ mile (sections 1-3, 5-7).

Maps: OS Landranger 197; Explorer 133 (and 134 for longer route only).

Start: GR 976215 main car park south of Market Square in Petworth. Petworth is on the junction of the A272, between Midhurst and Billingshurst, and the A283 between Chiddingfold and Pulborough.

Transport: Petworth is served by a variety of bus services from Horsham, Billingshurst, Midhurst and Pulborough.

Refreshments: the Stag Inn, Balls Cross; selection of pubs, teashops and restaurants in Petworth.

Introduction: This walk starts from the historic small town of Petworth, famous for Petworth House (National Trust) with its fine collection of paintings and sculpture and its extensive deer park. It is mainly through the West Sussex Low Weald of woods and fields but the first stretch out of the town takes the walker on a climb to Brinkshole Heath with widespread views of the South Downs, Black Down and the Surrey Hills, and the final stretch is through Petworth Park, landscaped by Capability Brown in the 18th century. Some of the unsurfaced bridleways can become muddy during wet weather; there are few stiles and no severe gradients.

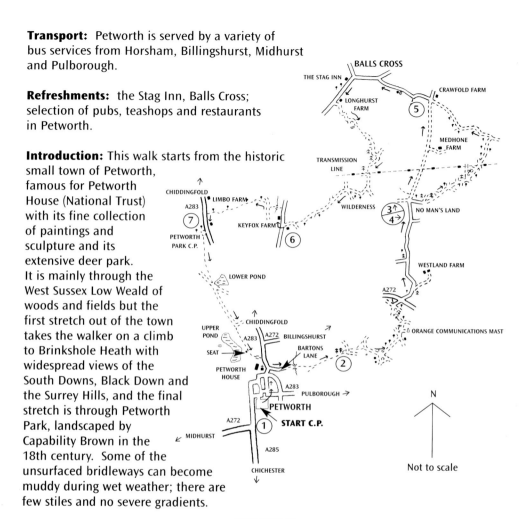

THE WALK

1. From the top of the car park near the entrance, with the toilet block on your right, go through the Old Bakery shopping arcade, leading out near the bottom of the town square (Market Square). Keep ahead, passing the United Reformed Church on your left, then cross to the right past New Street and continue uphill. In the corner follow the cobbled Lombard Street, still uphill. At the end, with the church gates ahead, turn right and then cross the road by an ornate lamp standard (take care) to George House. Turn left, go 20m/22yards and then turn right along Bartons Lane. In 100m/110yards, keep left (keeping the old stone wall on your left) and descend through a turnstile and then turn left again through a kissing gate. Continue straight downhill across the meadow to a small stone bridge; cross this and ascend, passing a gate in the corner to your left and making for the outer corner of a hedge. Continue uphill keeping the hedge on your left. Cross a stile ahead with a Serpent Trail waymark. In the next field,

continue forward uphill for 25m/28yards then start bearing left across the field towards a small clump of Scots pines on the summit (ignoring the fenced plantation of pine trees on your right with a Serpent Trail waymark). Pass these, keeping them on your left, and drop down to a stile. Cross this and continue uphill along an enclosed path.

2. At the top by the brown Leconfield Estate sign for Brinkshole Heath, turn right along the track and in 300m/330yards go over cross paths. In 20m/22yards at the next cross paths, where there is a view of buildings to your right and the Serpent Trail is waymarked ahead, turn left along a track with a solid rubble and gravel surface. Ignore all side turnings and eventually reach a junction with a driveway leading to houses on your right. Keep forward over this staggered crossing, soon passing a Water Board site and an Orange communications mast (and three others behind it) on your right and continue downhill through the wood, bearing right, until you reach a T-junction with a wide track. Turn right here and continue your descent to the A272 road. Cross the road taking care as this is a fast section, and go along a metalled road opposite (signs Public Bridleway and 'Oldham'). Continue on this road for about 1½km/1mile passing the entrance to Westland Farm, Pondtail (Cottage) and to Benefold Farm House on your right. Finally, 300m/330yards beyond the Benefold Farm House entrance, reach a crossing track (sign Public Bridleway). No Man's Land lies to your right between the farm entrance and the track.

3. **For the shorter route**, continue straight ahead on the farm track (bridleway) and keep to this, passing Medhone Farmhouse on your right. Reach a junction of tracks opposite cottages at Crawfold Farm (not signed) and turn left onto a surfaced track to rejoin the full route at section 5.

4. **To continue the longer route** turn right along another bridleway with a rubble and compressed soil surface, with fields to the right and woodland on the left. Soon after passing a field on the left, you reach a junction of five tracks by a fingerpost, and ignoring two to the right and another off left, keep forward on the main, surfaced, track. At the next junction of tracks, where the main track swings sharply left, keep ahead, staying on the signposted bridleway along an unsurfaced track. In about 300m/330yards pass under transmission lines, keeping ahead on the bridleway and avoiding a fork to the left and a path coming in from the right. In another 300m330yards, at a T-junction, turn left onto a broad vehicle track. After 200m/220yards turn right with the public bridleway, along a broad track, ignoring the grassy track also off right. Continue on it for 800m/½mile to a junction of tracks by cottages, with Crawfold Farm over to your right.

5. Go ahead, with the cottages on your right, along a metalled access road, and follow this as it swings left and then right, and continue for 800m/½mile to reach a public road. Turn left along it to Balls Cross and just beyond a road off to your right, reach the Stag Inn.

Continue on the road past the Inn. In 400m/¹/₄mile at Langhurst Farm turn left along a signed bridleway into a farmyard. At the far end of the yard, turn right with the bridleway along a cart track, and follow it for 400m/¹/₄mile to pass a pond and a track off right. Go forward here into a field with a hedge and a line of trees on your left. Enter a wood and keep straight ahead beyond a gate. Continue for 400/¹/₄mile, later keeping a field on your left, to a T-junction. Turn right and in another 150m/165yards keep left. At the transmission lines turn left and then immediately right. At the next junction of tracks in 200m/220yards, by a fingerpost, bear right, now with fields on your right and light woodland and a small pond on your left. After 300m/330yards, go straight over crossing paths (sign Public Bridleway). Continue through this woodland (Wilderness) for some 800m/¹/₂mile, keeping to the main track which starts with fields on your left and then bears right into an area of woodland on both sides; shortly afterwards there are fields on your right. There are two fingerposts (Public Bridleway) along this path (which can be very muddy after heavy rain), the first on your right and the second on your left. Finally leave the wood through a small gate and enter a field. Keeping the edge of the wood on your left, go uphill to the far corner of the field and through a field gate to bear right and then continue in the same direction along the track passing the farmyard to reach the road. Turn right along the road, passing Keyfox Farm on the left.

6. In 200m/220yards, turn left along a signed footpath across a stile and keep the hedge on your right. At the bottom of the dip, cross the footbridge and keep ahead. In 100m/110yards, at the top corner, go over a stile on your right and keep ahead along a field edge for 50m/55yards where, at a fingerpost, turn left and follow a field edge uphill with a wood on your right. At the top of the ascent turn left and then right, and enjoy the extensive views to the south. Descend and go through a small gate by a stile on your right. Turn left and cross the field diagonally to the next fingerpost, on the left of a small wood. Go over the stile by the gate and turn right to follow the footpath along the field edge and under power lines, to a stile on the right. Cross this to enter a wood and continue through the wood to reach the A283. Limbo and Limbo Farm lie just to your right here. Take care in crossing the road, turn left along the verge and then right to enter the Petworth Park National Trust car park.

7. From the information signboard in the top left hand corner, follow a well worn path southwards into the deer park. This path becomes a broad grassy track passing Lower Pond on your left. Keep ahead, bearing slightly right and gently ascend the ridge. Continue with the grassy track curving round to the left on higher ground where there are fine views of the South Downs and, close by, Upper Pond on your right. Bear right with this track and then left, continuing uphill to a stone seat under chestnut trees, where the façade of Petworth House is ahead. Keep forward to descend toward the ha-ha wall, go through an iron gate in the wall, and then through a short tunnel to enter the Cowyard. Bear right through it and out through the gate to the street. Cross this and turn right. Pass Christie's showroom and Bartons Lane and follow the road round to the right in front of the church. Just past the War Memorial turn left re-tracing your steps down cobbled Lombard Street to Petworth Market Square and on down to the car park.

19 Views and villages on the Sussex/Hampshire border – Queen Elizabeth Country Park, Buriton, and Chalton

Brian's walk

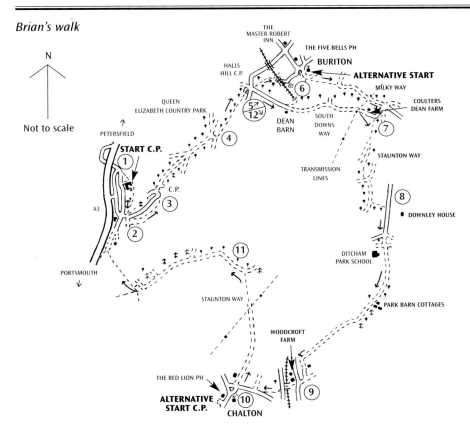

Length: 13¼km/8¼miles (sections 1-11) with a slightly shorter, less strenuous version avoiding Buriton, 13km/8miles (sections 1-4, 12 and 7-11).

Maps: OS Landranger 197 & 185; Explorer 120.

Start: GR 718186 Queen Elizabeth Country Park – main car park at the Visitor Centre, off the A3, 6½km/4miles south of Petersfield.

Alternative starts:
GR 740200 Buriton, roadside parking beside the church (start at section 6);
or GR 731159 Chalton car park, near the Red Lion PH (start at section 10).

Transport: Buses run from Petersfield to Buriton and along the A3 between Petersfield and Portsmouth, stopping close to the Country Park.

Refreshments: Queen Elizabeth Country Park Visitor Centre café; the Five Bells PH and the Master Robert Inn, Buriton; the Red Lion PH, Chalton.

Introduction: I really enjoy this walk as I appreciate a strenuous day out in country that has a pleasant mix of woods, farmland, downs, views and the picturesque villages associated with the Sussex/Hampshire countryside. From Buriton, it follows Buriton Hanger climbing the 'Milky Way' track (you will know why it has this name if wet). From the ridge above Downley and past Ditcham Park School there are glorious views across the Downs and from Chalton, you can see as far as Portsmouth and the Isle of Wight.

THE WALK

1. Start from the main car park. Facing the Visitor Centre turn left to the large and very distinctive fingerpost marked 'All Trails Start Here'. Turn right and follow the lower footpath waymarked 'South Downs Way' passing the Visitor Centre on your right. Follow the fingerpost marked 'Staunton Way' and 'Hangers Way' with the ecological pond on your right, the children's play area on your left and a large open field with picnic tables on your right. The Queen Elizabeth (QE) Country Park service road is on your right and gently curves to the left and crosses the path you are on. Follow the fingerpost 'South Downs Way – Walkers'.

2. At the road, cross diagonally left towards the footpath opening marked by a fingerpost 'Staunton Way'. Immediately turn left onto a footpath with a fingerpost 'South Downs Walkers and Hangers Way' which continues parallel to the road, passing an overflow car park on your left. The footpath continues through a wooded area to rejoin the road at a waymark where the road turns left, uphill. Enter the Benham Bushes car park and exit at the far end onto the forest maintenance vehicle track, with a fingerpost 'South Downs Way'.

3. Follow the forest track which rises gradually through wooded areas passing Benham Bushes barbecue site (picnic tables and shelter) on your right. Ignore the footpaths and tracks to your left and right, and continue ahead uphill following the yellow South Downs waymarks. Near the top of the hill, a forest maintenance vehicle track joins at a sharp angle from the right (fingerpost 'South Downs Way (Riders)'). Turn right onto this track.

4. After 100m/110yards, turn left off the track onto a footpath marked by a fingerpost 'Hangers Way'. Ignore the fingerpost 'South Downs Way' pointing in the opposite direction. The path descends through trees to a hedge and a kissing gate (waymarks 'Staunton Way' and 'Hangers Way'). In front is an open valley with views to the right of farming country. Continue through the kissing gate into a field along a path with a hedge and trees to your left, through a second kissing gate and across two fields with stiles into Halls Hill car park. *(If you wish to avoid Buriton and the steep descent and ascent, now go to section 12 and rejoin the walk at section 7.)*

5. Exit Halls Hill car park crossing a three way road junction to a footpath directly ahead into woods (fingerpost 'Bridle Path Hangers Way'). The path descends through woods with ancient quarries to your left and right. Ignore paths to your left and right and continue downhill passing under a railway bridge with Buriton Tunnel (railway) entrance above to your right. Pass a delightful thatched roof cottage, Whistlers, on your right and after a short distance arrive at Buriton village pond and church. This is an ideal spot for a short break or picnic. The village centre to your left (50m/55yards) has two pubs – the Five Bells and the Master Robert Inn.

6. Facing St Mary's Church, Buriton, with your back to the village pond, follow a fingerpost to a footpath to the right hand edge of the church wall. At a fingerpost, cross a stile into a field and immediately turn left (ignore the path ahead uphill) and continue along the field edge to another stile. With a hedge on your left, cross three fields with gates/stiles and exit into a farm lane which can be muddy at times - this is the 'Milky Way'. Turn right and follow the lane climbing uphill through woods and under transmission cables; from here there are excellent views of downland farming country. Continue to the road and ignoring the fingerpost 'South Downs Way', turn right along the road. After 200m/220yards, where the road turns sharp right, continue ahead onto a bridleway at a fingerpost 'Staunton Way' and enter Coulters Dean.

7. Follow the path which rises gently all the way with fields to right and woods to left, ignoring paths to your right and left. Leave Coulters Dean through a gate and continue on the bridleway which rises gently through woodland to a forest maintenance track. Cross the track onto the footpath waymarked 'Staunton Way' (the footpath may be overgrown) and follow this for about 100m/110yards to join another track by a waymark. Continue along the track with woodland to your right and a hedge with fields to your left for about 500m/550yards. The forest maintenance vehicle track continues ahead; turn left on to the bridleway waymarked 'Staunton Way'. Here again there are open fields to the right with views across downland and woodland to your left; continue along the bridleway until it joins a road at a fingerpost, and turn right along the road.

8. Continue along the road, with views of Downley House, a copse and a hanger to your left, until it bears right into Ditcham Park School. At this point there is a junction with a bridleway going off left and a track. Proceed ahead along the track (footpath 'Staunton Way') passing the school tennis courts on your right with views over farmland and the South Downs on your left and ahead. The track passes Park Barn Cottages and gardens on your left with fields to the right. Continue through woodland to emerge onto a grass track with open views to your left. Follow the track which gently descends to join the bridleway (waymark 'Staunton Way') alongside a cottage at the bottom of the hill and bear right to go onto a road.

9. Leave the Staunton Way which goes left. Cross the road into Woodcroft Farm with the notice 'Ditcham Park School Private Road' to your left. Follow the direction of the fingerpost along the track, keeping farm buildings to your right, towards a concrete railway footbridge. Cross the railway carefully but beware as the path exits immediately onto a quiet country road that has the occasional speeding car – so is potentially dangerous. On the road turn left and then right onto a footpath alongside a cottage garden (fingerpost Footpath). Follow the footpath steeply uphill crossing three stiles in open land into a field. *(To avoid this steep climb, continue along the road to the road junction and turn right to follow it as far as Chalton.)* Cross the field diagonally towards the left hedge and at the fingerpost, join the road and turn right to descend into the village of Chalton. At the road junction you can detour left to visit the Red Lion pub with its own car park alongside and the 700 year old church of St Michael and All Angels. The churchyard has some seats suitable for picnics. A public telephone and post box are all to your left and a small public car park is 25m/30yards past the pub on the right. Or, to continue the walk, turn right into a farmyard with a fingerpost (Staunton Way).

If starting from the car park here or leaving the pub, face the church and turn left (fingerpost *Staunton Way, QE Country Park*) to proceed past the village green, telephone and post box on your left, and go across the road into the farmyard ahead (fingerpost 'Staunton Way').

10. Keeping the farm buildings on your left, follow the concrete track which rises into a field and bear left through the hedge onto a farm track. Follow the track with the hedge on your right and extensive views across Hampshire on your left. Pass under electricity transmission cables towards the end of the hedge and, where the track turns right, keep straight along a footpath through a field going towards woods ahead.

11. Cross a stile into the woods (fingerpost 'QE Country Park') and turn left off the Staunton Way. Follow the 'Red Footprint' waymark with the Country Park on the right, and a hedge, wire fence and open views on your left. At the path junction, ignore the 'Red Footprint' waymark to the right and continue ahead keeping the hedge, fence and views on your left. Follow the main track until it reaches a T-junction. Then turn left downhill with a 'Red Horseshoe' waymark on your left. Continue with the hedge, fence and views on left, ignore the track to the right and follow ahead with 'Green Footprint' and 'Red Horseshoe' waymarks on your left. The track arrives at a corner of QE Country Park with a hedge on your left and ahead, having passed a 'Green Footprint' waymark on your left, the track bears right. Do not pass the 'Red Horseshoe' waymark, but turn left through the hedge, cross a stile onto a path and immediately turn right. Continue along the path with the QE Country Park on your right, and a fence, open fields and the noise from the A3 road beyond on your left. Continue ahead passing a fingerpost to your left and ignoring paths to the right. The footpath joins a farm track and now enters the QE Country Park; follow the track, with a works yard on your right and stables on your left, to a road. Follow the 'Blue Horseshoe' waymarks to go across the road onto a path passing a picnic area on your left to a footpath junction. At the fingerpost 'South Downs Way - Walkers', turn left and walk back to Visitor Centre and the main car park.

12. Less strenuous option: the walk can be shortened by about 400m/¹/₄mile cutting out 70m/200feet of descent and ascent; however, the picturesque village, duck pond, church and pubs of Buriton will be missed. To do so, complete the directions in sections 1-4 and then exit Halls Hill car park crossing the three way road junction onto the road, signposted 'Dean Barn 800m/¹/₂mile', and follow the direction of the fingerpost 'South Downs Way'. Continue along to Dean Barn where the road finishes in a gravel surfaced car park and turning area. Join the farm track ahead (fingerpost 'South Downs Way') and continue through undulating country under electricity transmission cables until the track changes to a road at Coulters Dean Farm. After 100m/110yards or so, where the road makes a sharp left turn, turn right onto a bridleway at the fingerpost 'Staunton Way' and enter Coulters Dean. To complete the walk, pick up the directions in sections 7 to 11 which will take you back to the car park.

20 Three in One on the South Downs - Cocking, Charlton and Singleton

Kate C's walk

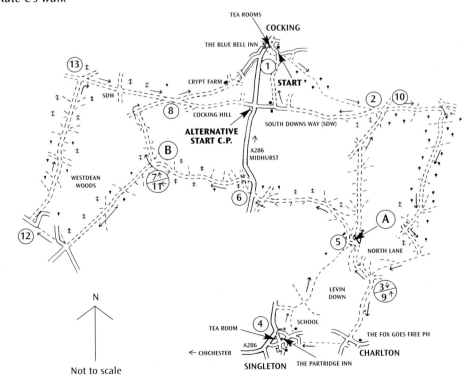

Length: The main walk is 17¹/₂km/11miles (sections 1-8) but other variations are possible (see sketch map). Two shorter walks of either 15¹/₂km/9¹/₂miles (sections 1-4, 9 [point A] and 10) **or** 11km/7miles* (sections 1, 2, 9 [point A] and 10) are described, as well as a longer walk of 22km/14miles (sections 1-6, 11-13 and 8). (*Note: 12¹/₄km/8miles to include the pub at Charlton – see map)

Maps: OS; Landranger 197; Explorer 120 & 121.

Start: GR 879175 the lane below Cocking Church.
On entering Cocking village on the A286 from the north, take the left turn (marked To Church) then go immediately right downhill to park below the church.

Alternative start: GR 875166 car park at the top of Cocking Hill on the A286 Midhurst/Chichester road at the South Downs Way (SDW) crossing. From here cross the road, go along the SDW as far as the first crossing path and then follow the directions from section 2, keeping forward on the SDW – see map.

Transport: buses run from Bognor, Chichester and Midhurst via Cocking and Singleton.

Refreshments: the Blue Bell Inn and Moonlight Cottage Tea Rooms, Cocking; the Fox Goes Free PH, Charlton: the Partridge Inn and the Studio Tea Room, Singleton.

Introduction: The South Downs is one of my favourite walking areas, for the wonderful views and variety, particularly from Cocking and Singleton. There is an abundance of wild flowers around for most of the year and on a clear day it is possible to see the sea and the Isle of Wight. While there are a number of hills to climb on this walk, the effort is always rewarded by wonderful views and of course they make excellent exercise! Please note that care will be needed on the chalky paths and tracks which can be very slippery when wet.

THE WALK

Main Walk 17¹/₂km/11miles

1. With your back to the church, take the road round to the left to a fingerpost in the hedgerow (with steps and a stile) on the right (50m/55yards). Cross the stile into a field and head diagonally left to go into next field through a gap in the hedge and follow the hedgerow on your right uphill until the footpath enters a wood through a gate. Continue uphill through the wood to reach the Downs, (take heart, this is the steepest hill of the whole walk, but the views are worth it when you reach the top!). At the top, cross the stile into a field and continue slightly left diagonally to another stile into a large field and continue in the same direction heading for the left edge of the forest seen ahead, toward the far right hand corner of the field. Just before reaching the corner, bear right to reach the South Downs Way (SDW) at a five armed fingerpost.

2. Take the SDW to the left passing two crossing paths and take the bridleway to the right at the third crossed paths. Follow this bridleway downhill through woods (fingerposts indicate direction) passing several fire breaks until you reach a T-junction at a wide gravel track. Turn right following the track down for a short distance to a small building on the right and a metal gate ahead. Go through the gate and immediately take the footpath left uphill (the fingerpost is off the path on the right). Crossing over two fire breaks continue on to reach a broken gate just before a crossing footpath sign. Take the right hand path over a stile into a field and follow the marked path in a diagonally right direction across the field to a waymark post. Continue in the same direction towards a second waymark post where you turn right keeping parallel with the edge of the field for about 100m/110yards and then bear left across to a stile (and another waymark post) which takes you into a field. (Crops may make this stile difficult to see, but it is there!) Cross the field, keeping the scrub on your left, down to a broken stile, and then keep ahead and sharply down between brambles to a stile and a metal gate to join a chalk track (North Lane). **For the shorter walk of 11km/7miles go to section 9 – see map.**

3. Follow the track left to the road, cross this to go down the road opposite (signposted 'Goodwood 1') and very shortly take the footpath on the right across the field and through a kissing gate into Singleton village. Follow the footpath signs in the same direction, as the path goes through the houses, until it joins a farm road just after the Church. Bear right down the road which brings you out opposite the village pub (The Partridge). Cross straight over and continue down the road beside the pub wall to reach a road junction. The tea room is on the left, on the corner facing the A286.

4. At the junction, turn right to take the minor road to Charlton bearing left along the road to reach a footpath sign beside the village school. Turn left and follow the path between fences past the graveyard and then up the hill to cross a stile onto Levin Down. Ignore the obvious track to the right and keep ahead; in a short distance the path meets a bridleway at a three-armed fingerpost. Turn right and follow the bridleway uphill ignoring the crossing footpath to pass through a gate. There is no clear path but keep forward uphill over the rise of the Down where, on a clear day, the Isle of Wight may be seen. Continue downhill heading to a gate in a fence just before a crossroad of paths. Go through the gate. **(Point A) For the shorter walk of 15$\frac{1}{2}$km/9$\frac{1}{2}$miles, follow the instructions from Point A in section 9, then 10.**

5. To continue the main route, take the bridleway to the left of a National Trust sign 'Drovers Estate' **(Point A)** going through a small gate; this drops straight down over a grassy hill to the back of a farm. Pass through a farm gateway, keeping the same direction and, leaving the farm on the left, follow the bridleway as it climbs between hedges. Continue along the bridleway and in approximately 400m/$\frac{1}{4}$mile, the path bears right through woods for about 800m/$\frac{1}{2}$mile. Be careful not to miss the waymarker post with a blue arrow under trees on the right at the bottom of a slope where the path bends to the left. Bear right here and keep ahead until you reach a tarmac road; turn left for a short distance and then follow a path on the right that will take you quite sharply downhill, eventually to join the A286.

6. Cross the road carefully to a permissive bridleway opposite. Keeping parallel to the road continue right along this, to reach a T-junction with a bridleway on the right leading in from the road. Turn left here; the bridleway leads uphill, bearing left over a bridge, a relic of the old railway from Chichester to Midhurst. Immediately, at a Y-junction, branch left onto a grassy track heading west which eventually passes through woods - great at bluebell time! Keep ahead at the crossing track where there is a fingerpost in trees on your left and after about 700m/770yards, the path joins another gravel track. Bear left on this track which comes out into a clearing where there is usually wood cutting industry in progress. On the far side of the clearing, find a three-fingered footpath sign on the left. **(Point B)** **To continue the long walk, go to section 11 – see map.**

7. Take the path to the right uphill through the woods. Very soon, take the left branch and continue up to a T-junction at the edge of woods. Take the right hand path to the SDW.

8. Cross over to the fields opposite and follow the bridleway down through a small wood into Crypt Farm. Passing the stable block on your right, follow the drive beside a stream down to the A286 and cross over with care to a footpath beside the tea rooms which leads you back down to Cocking Church.

Short Walk – 11km/7 miles

Follow the directions in sections 1 and 2. *If you wish to visit the pub in Charlton, follow the track (North Lane) left to the road, turn left to reach the Fox Goes Free and then retrace your steps to this point.*

9. On reaching North Lane, turn right up the lane and then take the left fork up a chalk road and on to crossing paths ahead to reach **Point A** (National Trust sign 'Drovers Estate' between a three-armed fingerpost and gate to the left and a four-armed fingerpost to the right). Go right to the four-armed fingerpost, turn left and take the bridleway just beyond the sign and follow this between fences heading north into woods where there are wild flowers in abundance. Continue uphill for $2^1/_2$km/$1^1/_2$miles, ignoring all crossing tracks, until the path reaches the SDW at the top.

10. Turn left along the SDW, covering a short distance first walked on your outward journey, to continue downhill in a westerly direction until you reach farm buildings. Turn right after Manor Farm and take the bridleway downhill to join the road below Cocking Church; this is a rough track but you will reach the church in about 20 minutes. The footpath on your left as you reach the parking spot will take you up to the tea rooms, should you want refreshment after your walk.

Long Walk – 22km/14miles

11. Follow the directions in sections 1-6. At the three fingered footpath sign **(Point B)**, take the left path (bridleway), south west downhill through woods, passing a charcoal burners' work area. When reaching the open fields (about 1km/²/₃mile) carry on with the woods on your right until the bridleway exits onto a road through a gate. Turn right along the road for 100m/110yards. Where the road bears right, take the footpath leading off left up through a copse, go over a stile and into fields to continue ahead until you reach another road at a bend.

12. Stay ahead on the road briefly then turn right (fingerpost) into a field through a gate, and pass up the left side of the field to reach another gate. Keeping ahead, this track eventually enters Westdean woods where in February/March wild daffodils may be found. Ignore all paths to right or left until you arrive at the top of the hill (crossed tracks) then turn right onto the SDW, a distance of about 2km/1¼miles.

13. Follow the SDW east and at the highest point on the path ahead spare a moment to turn round and enjoy the view - on a good day you will be able to see the Isle of Wight. **Rejoin the main walk at section 8** at the second crossed paths, just over 800m/¹/₂mile away, by turning left to the fields to follow the bridleway downhill.

21 Rambles in the Rother Valley – Lavington Common, Selham, Tillington and Heath End

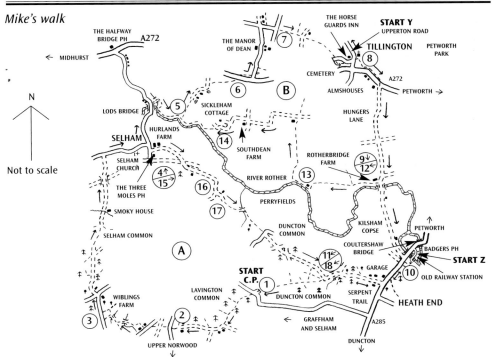

Mike's walk

Not to scale

Length: 15km/9¼miles for a long circular walk towards Petworth (sections 1-11); start at **X, Y or Z**. Two shorter circuits are possible - see sketch map.
Circuit A goes south of the Rother (sections 1-3, 15-18), 9½km/6miles (12km/7½miles to include Badgers PH or the Old Railway Station; start at **X**. **Circuit B**, goes north of the Rother (sections 8, 12-14, 5-7) 9½km/6miles or 12½km/8miles to include the Three Moles PH at Selham; start at **Y**.

Maps: OS Landranger 197; Explorer 133 & 121.

Start: GR 949187 (**X**) National Trust (NT) car park at Lavington Common.
From the A285 from Petworth to Duncton, take the minor road signed to Graffham and Selham. The car park is 1½km/1mile along the road on the right hand side.

Alternative starts: GR 962223 (**Y**) north of Tillington on Upperton Road; walk downhill to Tillington Church and follow sections 8-11, 1-7. Turn off the A272 into Tillington, west of Petworth, just after the end of the walls of Petworth Park.
or GR 971192 (**Z**) by Badgers PH (but not in their car park) on the station approach, south of Petworth and follow sections 10, 11, 1-9. Badgers is on the A285 2½km/1½miles south of Petworth, shortly after Coultershaw Bridge.

Transport: Buses between Petworth and Midhurst stop at Tillington; those between Petworth and Chichester pass Badgers and the Old Railway Station on the A285.

Refreshments: the Three Moles PH, Selham (note: no food served); the Horse Guards Inn and Restaurant, Tillington; Badgers PH and restaurant, the Old Railway Station both near Coultershaw Bridge, south of Petworth. The Halfway Bridge PH and restaurant on A272 north of Lods Bridge is ½km/550yards from the route (section 4).

Introduction: This walk offers several options all of which give varied walking in woodland, farmland and heathland along the Rother Valley. It is mostly on footpaths, bridleways and lanes, and includes the old stagecoach route and smugglers' track to the coast. This is an excellent springtime walk with possibly every local native wild flower. In autumn, Kilsham Copse, Duncton Common and other National Trust (NT) areas have a proliferation of colourful fungi.
NB: The lowland areas adjoining the river Rother used in section 14 of Circuit B, the short walk north of the Rother, can be very wet at any time of serious flooding, so do check the state of the river before undertaking the walk which uses the water meadows and lowland farm pasture areas.

THE WALK

Long circular walk 15km/9¼miles

1. From the car park at **X**, cross the road and go through a kissing gate to enter Lavington Plantation (NT), an area being actively managed to restore it to heathland. Keep to the footpath straight ahead across the common for 400m/¼mile, ignoring all other paths and tracks, until you reach a kissing gate and cottages. At the end of the cottages, go through the metal gate; the footpath bears right to be joined by another footpath (gravel road) coming from the left. Continue on the same track to pass between an

estate office on the left and farm machinery buildings to the right. Go ahead keeping the buildings on your left along a footpath that now enters polo training grounds. Then it leaves the track and goes straight on to run alongside a fenced field to the left, with woodland to the right. Stay on this footpath and cross a stile to go between wire fences with horse paddocks to both sides. Before a stable block cross a further stile and take the track directly opposite the line of the path. *Do not take the left track.* The line of the footpath follows this track to curve right and rise to join the lane to Upper Norwood.

2. Cross the lane to join the footpath immediately opposite beside a drive to a house. Continue forward to the top of the rise where the path meets a farm track. Go straight ahead crossing a stile into a field. *Do not take the stile on the right.* The path drops down through the field to a further stile. Cross this stile and turn left on to a lane. After 50m/55yards turn right onto a footpath between cottages, following the line of the path around a large garden to the left and then a field on the right. Follow this field boundary round to the right. Go into a small wood with a stream meandering though it; keeping at the higher level, follow the stream to a bridge. Go over the bridge and cross the stile at the top of the bank into a field. Walk up to the hill-crest of this field, then drop down towards a gate where another footpath comes in from the left. Go through the gate into a small meadow, continue past the large oak tree to another gate; go through this, cross a small bridge over the brook and enter a copse. In spring, this area is a carpet of wild daffodils. At the top of the short rise ignore the footpath coming in from the left and, keeping to the right, continue for 75m/80yards turning left at the next footpath. This area is mostly thin coppice and is full of spring flowers. Keep on this footpath bearing left (west) to join a lane. Turn right onto the lane heading downhill.

3. Stay on the lane, now heading north to pass Wiblings Farm on the right, until you reach a road junction. Take care at the blind corner! Cross at the junction to a bridleway immediately opposite, passing a large dwelling called Shrublands to the right. Stay on the bridleway as it rises up to woodland. At the top ignore the paths left and right and stay on the bridleway through the pine wood initially running parallel to the Serpent Trail. After 400m/¼mile the bridleway leaves the wood through a gate into a field. Go ahead past a large tree and descend towards the Rother valley with fine views ahead to the north-west. Head for the green barn and stay on the bridleway passing Smoky House. This is now Smokyhouse Lane which passes over the old Petersfield to Horsham railway line. Continue along it for 800m/½mile to reach a road. Turn right along the road and in 800m/½mile pass Selham Church, reported to have been raided by the Vikings. Continue to a T-junction.

If you wish to have an early refreshment stop, turn right to take the road to the Three Moles PH (250m/275yards) and afterwards retrace your steps to the T-junction.

If you are taking Circuit A south of the Rother, go to section 15 for instructions to continue your route.

4. Turn left along the minor road towards Lods Bridge for 800m/½mile, taking care, especially on the blind bend. Immediately after crossing the bridge go over the stile on the right and cross the field diagonally to a further bridge. Cross this bridge, go through the gate and turn right into a large meadow with the River Rother to the right. The footpath follows the bank of the river to the far end of this meadow. Pass through the narrow opening, sometimes gated, into a further meadow, still with the river to the right. Stay on the line of the footpath beside the riverbank for 20m/22yards. Turn left and north onto the raised field bank and cross a stile, where there is a good view towards Bexley Hill on the left, onto a field edge footpath with a copse to the right.

5. Continue on the footpath keeping to the field edge to go over a further stile. Pass a pond to the right with a hedgerow to your left and eventually a brick/flint wall to the right. At the end of the wall and farmhouse, go through the gate, continue straight on to leave the path and join a farm lane passing barns to the right to reach a lay-by/gate. Go though this gate and turn immediately right onto a field edge footpath. Keep to the right hand side of the field and stay on this path along the field boundary until you cross a stile out to the A272 Midhurst to Petworth road.

6. Cross the road, taking considerable care as it is often busy. On the opposite bank, go through a gate and turn right to join a pathway that runs east, the line of the original road. Stay on this path until you reach a lane. Turn left onto the lane, heading up the hill to pass the Manor of Dean (the garden is often open to the public under the National Gardens Scheme) on your right and continue until you reach a crossroads. At the junction turn right onto another lane; continue up a slight rise, ignoring all other paths, to pass Dene Dip with metal railings to the left. At the end of this lane you come to a further lane (New Road). Cross to a footpath opposite heading between fields with views to the South Downs to the right.

7. Continue ahead on this footpath. Go through a gate, crossing a sunken track. In about 200m/220yards, the footpath turns downhill slightly towards the village of Tillington, with the unusual church tower clearly visible ahead. The footpath ends at a lane immediately opposite a set of gates to the parish cemetery. Go through the gates to join a path between an avenue of trees. After a short distance turn left onto the path running up through the centre of the cemetery. Go through the lych gate ahead straight on into a lane (Cemetery Lane) with cottages on both sides, and pass the Old Manor House on the right. Go forward to join a footpath to the left which rises above the lane and turns left to pass the Horse Guards Inn and Restaurant. This is now Upperton Road, Tillington. Where the railings end, turn right to cross the road to Tillington Church.

8. Take the path up beside and beyond the church where there are excellent views to the South Downs. Turn left and continue through the churchyard to the wall ahead, turn right and go down a short flight of steps. Stay on this footpath with the wall to Petworth Park to the left to rejoin the A272 Midhurst to Petworth Road.

At the road, continue ahead keeping the Park wall to your left and stay on the pavement path for 400m/^{1}/$_4$mile yards. Cross the road to walk downhill along a green lane to the left of an old Almshouse/former lodge gatehouse. This is Hungers Lane (no sign), which was once the coach road to Chichester and is reputed to be an old smugglers' way, as well as being haunted by an elderly man. It is host to badgers' setts (all year) and snowdrops in springtime. Stay on this lane for 1^1/$_4$km/1mile crossing over the farm road, where it becomes a bridleway. At the end of the sunken path, keep straight on as the bridleway joins a metalled farm track/drive towards Rother Bridge. **For circuit B, go to sections 12-14.**

9. Cross the bridge onto a farm track - the continuation of the bridleway. After passing a pair of cottages to the left, the bridleway surface is a partly metalled farm road. Keep on for 1^1/$_4$km/^{3}/$_4$mile ignoring all sidetracks. Towards the end of the bridleway/road, as it rises to meet the A285 Petworth to Duncton Road, there are splendid views down to the Rother below. The track joins the road between the river and the old disused Petersfield to Horsham railway.

For refreshment, turn left here for Badgers PH and restaurant or to visit the Old Railway Station with its former Orient Express railway carriages where teas and coffees are available. ***This can also serve as an alternative start (Z)*** *but adds to the length of Circuit A.*

10. Turn right on the A285 to cross the old railway bridge, taking care on a very busy main road, where there is no footpath for 30m/33yards. Cross to the other side of the road to the footpath beside the road, running uphill for 400m/^{1}/$_4$mile to a fingerpost (Public Bridleway). Re-cross the road to walk along a track/bridleway immediately after the garage on the right, pass cottages on the left and continue ahead. Walk around the metal gate and enter Kilsham Copse. Go straight on along the bridleway, which soon goes down through pine woods. After about 800m/^{1}/$_2$mile from the road, cross a stream, and very shortly the track forks, (sign for the Serpent Trail). This is now Duncton Common.

11. Take the footpath branching off left (sign for the Serpent Trail) that starts to rise and after 100m/110yards crosses a further footpath. Keep straight on about 800m/^{1}/$_2$mile, ignoring all other tracks to enter the NT owned heathland through wooden barriers, keeping to the same line. Continue along the footpath for 300m/330yards following a low raised causeway across the heathland to a lane where you turn right to return to the car park.

Circuit B (north of the Rother) 9^1/$_2$km/6miles

This walk starts on Upperton Road, north of Tillington (Y). From your parking place, walk down the road towards the A272 until you reach the church. From here, follow the narrative in section 8, then sections 12-14 and 5-7. (NB. Check the level of the river Rother before doing this circuit.)

12. At Rotherbridge Farm, just before you reach the bridge to cross the river Rother, turn right at the waymarker post in front of the farmhouse. Go past a barn on the right and over the stile into a narrow field with the river on your left. Follow this path beside the hedge past a gate, a footpath and a second gate on the right. Go over a stile beside the third gate and follow the footpath between hedges for about 400m/¼mile. The path emerges from between the hedges with a barn ahead, Perryfields. Take the path to your left and after a short distance, bear right to go behind the barns and then through a metal gate. Continue on this path until you reach the bottom of a downhill section, then turn right just in front of a metal gate.

13. Follow this path northwards, ignoring a crossing track, until it meets an unmetalled farm road; there is a small derelict stone barn on the left hand corner. (Access to the next section is allowed through the DEFRA Countryside Stewardship Scheme - see signs). Turn left onto this farm road to cross the field, then turn left and follow the boundary hedge for a short distance before turning right to reach Southdean Farm. Turn right beside a garden to the farmhouse and almost immediately turn left into the farmyard. Go ahead taking the footpath which leaves the far side of the farmyard in the right hand corner. Follow the sunken path between hedges as it zigzags around the garden to Sickleham Cottage and drops down through a small wood towards the river. You emerge from the wood into a very marshy meadow. *This area is a wildlife habitat and is usually very wet and sometimes becomes flooded after heavy rainfall.*

14. Follow short sections of the boarded walkway. After the second section (10m/11yards) turn right continuing across sections of boardwalk and then carefully pick your way through this very marshy area. In about 150m/165yards you will reach the riverbank. Turn right, follow the riverbank and leave the marshy section by crossing a stile on top of the riverbank into a long narrow meadow. Follow the riverbank around the perimeter of the meadow. After passing through a post and wire fence where the meadow narrows, you will see on the raised bank to the right a gate with a stile beside it.

If you wish to visit the Three Moles PH, (1½km/1mile) continue beside the river through a narrow neck of land into a large meadow. Follow the field edge for about 400m/¼mile, until you come to a field entrance on the left. Go through this entrance and over the stone bridge into a small field. Go diagonally across this field to cross a stile onto the road adjoining a bridge over the Rother. Turn left over this bridge and follow the road, taking great care on the blind bend immediately after the bridge, to the Three Moles. After your refreshments, return in reverse by the route described above to continue the walk.

Go over the stile, and then follow the instructions for the long walk in sections 5 - 7 to return to Upperton Road, Tillington near the church.

Circuit A (south of the Rother) 9¹/₂km/6miles

15. Follow sections 1 to 3 of the long walk. At the T-junction turn right into the road towards the Three Moles PH and almost immediately turn left into a farmyard area (Hurlands Farm) between the group of farm cottages. *(Should you wish to stop at the pub, continue a little further along the road and then retrace your steps to this point.)* Take the farm road straight ahead between the barns, heading east, into open country. The road continues between hedgerows gradually bearing right until it reaches the line of the former Horsham to Petersfield railway. This road is extremely muddy during and after wet weather. Pass through the collapsed arch of a railway bridge, turn left passing barns on your right and continue ahead on the pathway keeping the railway embankment on your left. *This next section of the path is extremely wet following rain.*

16. After about 300m/330yards, turn right and follow the farm track between the hedges. On reaching the next junction, go straight ahead, crossing a stile beside the entrance to a converted barn. Go on through the gate into a field and at end of the garden, go over another stile into the field behind the house. Be sure to enter the field on the left-hand side of the hedgerow that heads east behind the house.

17. Follow the field edge keeping the hedgerow and bank on your right. There are good views towards Tillington from this point. Near the end of the field, go into a small copse and drop down to cross a brook and stile into a small meadow. Go over the bridge ahead, turn right for 20m/22yards and then cross another stile into a wood. Follow the line of the stream through the wood. In a short distance, when the footpath leaves the line of the stream and climbs slowly in a narrow copse between two fields, continue along it for about 400m/¹/₄mile. As you enter a conifer wood you meet a metalled farm track. Turn left and then almost immediately right up a bridleway that climbs through the pine wood and on through an area of rhododendrons. On reaching a cross path, turn left through a gap in a bank and immediately right as indicated by the fingerpost. Keep straight ahead on the waymarked bridleway ignoring other paths as it continues up a gentle rise onto a common. In a short distance the bridleway descends on a sunken track between an open field on the left and the common on the right. This is Duncton Common. At the next cross-path, go ahead and shortly you will meet a double 'Y' junction.

Should you wish to visit Badgers or the Old Railway Station (1¹/₂km/1mile each way) before continuing the walk, go ahead to cross a bridge over a small fast moving stream and follow the main track (Serpent Trail markers) up through the woods. In 400m/¹/₄mile go through an iron gate and continue along the track until you reach a road (A285). Cross the road, turn left and follow the pavement downhill to a narrow road bridge. (There is no footpath here for the next 100m/110yards so take great care.) Cross this and the river bridge, keep close to the hedge and in about 80m/88yards you will come to Badgers PH. The Old Railway Station where teas and coffees are served is a short distance along the access road in front of the PH. After refreshment, retrace your steps to continue the walk back to Lavington Common at section 18.

18. Turn right at this point onto the second footpath, signed 'Serpent Trail'. The footpath starts to rise and after 100m/110yards crosses a further footpath. Keep straight on ignoring all other tracks until you reach the NT owned heathland after about 800m/$\frac{1}{2}$mile where you enter the heath access land through wooden barriers. Keeping to the same line follow a low raised causeway for 300m/330yards across the heathland to a lane. Turn right for a short distance to return to the NT car park on Lavington Common.

22 Panorama of the Downs - Kithurst Hill, Houghton, Burpham and Chantry Post

Olive's walk

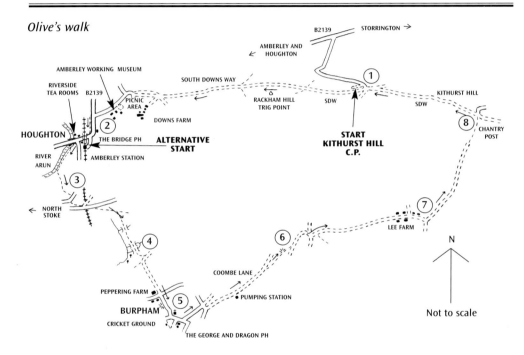

Length: 17km/10$\frac{1}{2}$miles.

Maps: OS Landranger 197; Explorer 121.

Start: GR 070124 Kithurst Hill car park.
This is on the South Downs Way (SDW) at the top of a lane leading off the B2139 Storrington/Houghton road about 5km/3miles east of Amberley station.

Alternative start: GR 027118 Amberley station, near Houghton Bridge.
Walk down to the road (B2139) cross over, turn left and start the walk at section 2.

Transport: Amberley station is on the London Victoria/Bognor Regis/Chichester line. Buses from Pulborough, Storrington, Chichester and Horsham pass the station and Amberley Working Museum, a short distance from it. Start the walk at section 2.

Refreshments: the George and Dragon PH, Burpham; the Bridge Inn and the Houghton Bridge Riverside Tea Rooms, Houghton.

Introduction: This is a beautiful downland walk that starts and finishes on the top of the South Downs so there are many wide and open views. Particularly special are the views of Parham House as you start, Amberley Castle and the Wildbrooks as you approach Downs Farm and nearing Burpham, Arundel Castle across the river.

THE WALK

1. From the top of the lane, go through the side access beside the metal gates and turn right onto a broad track. This is the South Downs Way (SDW), identified on the fingerpost with an acorn symbol to indicate a National Trail. Follow these signs for approximately 3km/2miles, forking right at a junction, go past the trig point at Rackham Hill, and continue to reach a major footpath junction at the foot of the slope, with a large cluster of farm buildings (Downs Farm - no sign) on your left ahead of you. This is a very straightforward, yet attractive part of the walk, with many open views, and particularly beautiful ones of Amberley and the Wildbrooks from about half way along. After passing through the small five-bar gate, continue along the SDW, by taking the narrow path half right, with fencing either side, going downhill to meet a lane. On meeting the lane, turn right for about 20m/22yards to the Y-junction. Turn left continuing downhill on the SDW towards Amberley station. *(Part way down, by turning in on the left, you will find a very nice grassy area that makes an excellent picnic stop overlooking the Amberley Working Museum. It also offers some shelter if required).* At the bottom, cross the B2139 with care and turn left along the footpath beside this busy road towards Houghton Bridge, passing both the Museum and the station on your left.

2. Go under the railway bridge to reach Houghton Bridge crossing the river Arun. This is a very pretty area, with two opportunities for refreshments here and the possibility of a boat trip in summer. Half way over the bridge, cross over the road (taking great care as it is very busy) to a footpath on the left, go over a stile and follow the track a short way to a further stile. Continue along this footpath on the dyke on the left hand side of the river to a stile ahead of you. Cross this stile, and after about 70m/77yards, turn left to climb a stile onto a narrow footpath in a lightly wooded area, which can be very muddy in wet weather. Follow this for about 400m/¼mile to a five-bar gate and the lane to the north of the village of North Stoke.

3. Turn right onto the lane for about 100m/110yards, passing the first gate into a caravan field. Go through the second

gate on your left, turn into the field and bear right up the bank to follow a small path through trees above the field. Continue for about 300m/330yards going gently uphill and, when the path opens out, make sure you continue straight ahead to rejoin the lane. At the lane turn left to cross over the railway bridge, passing a wildlife sign on the left. Turn right after about 25m/28yards to go through a gate hidden by the hedge onto a field path (bridleway) which crosses the hillside diagonally, and reach a field gate at the bottom. Go through this and in just 10m/11yards, turn right over a stile into the wooded area. Follow this narrow path which twists and turns for some 500m/550yards. Shortly after crossing the *second* footbridge, turn left to cross a stream and stile into a field; walk along the right hand edge to a T-junction with an old quarry face (or chalk cliff) ahead of you.

4 Turn right to follow the bridleway up to Peppering Farm, ignoring the path to the right. At the farm you will find crossing lanes; keep forward along the middle lane for about 600m/660yards to reach Burpham. As you walk along this lane enjoy the views to the right across the valley where you will see Arundel Castle in the distance. You are now approximately halfway through the walk. At the end of this lane turn left, and shortly afterwards reach the George and Dragon pub on the right. The church of St Mary the Virgin, almost opposite, is worth a visit if you can spare the time. There is a cricket pitch just beyond the pub which makes a good picnic spot.

5. Take the lane downhill from the pub to go through the village, turning left opposite Pensway Cottage, to follow the main road. At a T-junction with a broad track ahead turn right downhill, still on the main road, and shortly afterwards take the first turning left, Coombe Lane. Go along here passing a house, Coombe Cottage, and keep ahead on a green lane with a pumping station over to the right. Partway along the green lane, you come to a five-bar gate where the landscape opens up and you can see the Downs ahead of you. Continue on the bridleway with the fence on the left hand side, until you reach a fingerpost and here bear right on the footpath which goes off uphill. At the top of the first rise, go over a stile *and continue uphill in the same direction* across a field towards a fingerpost on the skyline. This is the only steep gradient in the walk. As you steadily climb make sure you look back to appreciate some of the best views on this walk.

6. When you reach a gravelled farm track, turn left. Follow this track as it swings round to the right and joins a bridleway at the start of a concrete track. Here turn right and then almost immediately left on the concrete roadway. Follow this, which now becomes a chalky track for approximately 1¹/₂km/1mile, and go through the farmyard at Lee Farm. Continue on this track passing residential houses and barns.

7. At the bottom of the hill where the main track swings right, go forward through the left hand gate and bear left on a bridleway. Follow this, keeping a fence on your left heading gently uphill for about 2km/1¹/₄miles to Chantry Post, to rejoin the SDW.

8. Turn left onto the SDW, heading west again for another1¹/₂km/1mile to return to the car park.

23 Through history in the Adur Valley - Ashurst, Bramber, and Henfield

Jane's walk

Length: Two circular walks from Ashurst.
Walk A (17¹/₂km/11miles) goes south via Bramber (sections 1-9).

Walk B (17¹/₂km/11miles) goes east via Henfield (sections 1-4, 10-16, 8 and 9) and can be shortened to 11km/6³/₄miles (sections 1-4, 10, 8, 9).

Maps: OS Landranger 198; Explorer 122.

Start: GR 176160 Ashurst Recreation Ground. Take the B2135 which runs between the A24 (south of A272 crossing) and the A283 Steyning bypass. In Ashurst, turn into School Lane. The recreation ground is 400m/¹/₄mile along on the left just before reaching the school.

Alternative starts: - for Walk A GR 185106 Bramber Castle car park off the roundabout at the eastern end of the A283, Steyning bypass. Go down to the entrance to the car park and start at section 6.

or for Walk B GR 214161 the Library car park, Henfield High Street (the A281). Walk to the High Street, turn left and then turn into Church Street immediately past the traffic lights. Start at section 15.

Transport: Henfield and Bramber are served by buses from Horsham, Worthing, Brighton and Burgess Hill but the service to Ashurst is very restricted.

Refreshments: the Fountain Inn, Ashurst; the Castle Hotel, Bramber; the Bridge Inn and the Kings Head PH, Upper Beeding; the White Hart PH, the George Hotel and a variety of cafés and restaurants in Henfield High Street.

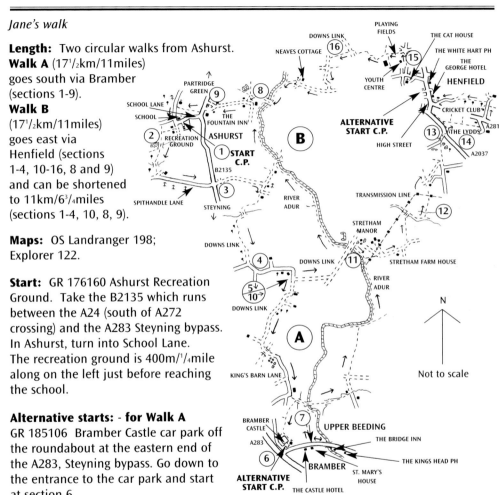

Introduction: I love to walk beside the river Adur; these walks include flat stretches along its banks and the surrounding water meadows as well as varied gently undulating farmland. They are beautiful walks in dry conditions, but in wet weather, and very often in the winter, some of the terrain will be very muddy. Some of the water meadows are impassable in the wettest of the winter months. During the walks I can often spot deer, and a large variety of birds, especially on the water meadows and the river. One walk goes through Henfield, an attractive village with some interesting old buildings, and the other offers an opportunity to visit the ruins of Bramber Castle and the adjacent church.

THE WALK

Walk A – (via Bramber) 17¹/₂km/11miles

1. Turn left out of the car park into School Lane and walk a short distance along the road, passing the school on your right, until the road turns sharply to the right. Turn left by a house called Burnetts and walk ahead onto a gravelled track through the gates of Sweethill Farm. Turn right onto a concrete track between two barns (fingerpost Public Footpath) and go ahead to cross the stile beside the metal gate ahead of you. Do stop to admire the wonderful view of Chanctonbury Ring to your left! Continue across the field slightly diagonally to your left to the end of the field and turn left, crossing the stile and going downhill towards woods.

2. Go across a small footbridge over a stream with a small weir on the right, and go straight on keeping the fence on your right. Ignore the path going off on your right and continue straight ahead. Cross another small footbridge and leaving the mixed woodland on your right, almost immediately cross another stile into a field on your left with a house ahead of you, also to the left. Keep straight ahead beside the woodland on your right. At the end of the field, cross another stile and turn right and go onto a gravelled road until you come to a track to the tarmac road ahead (Spithandle Lane). Turn left and continue along Spithandle Lane for about 800m/¹/₂mile, walking on the verges wherever possible, until you reach a main road (B2135).

3. Go straight across the road, taking care as this can be a busy section, and take the metalled farm lane, signed Public Bridleway, to the right of the sign for Ashurst Place Farm. Follow this lane/bridleway for about 500m/550yards until it passes this farm and shortly afterwards as the track divides, turn right in front of a house. Follow the lane/bridleway a short distance until it bears left and now take the footpath straight on through a gate into the farmyard and immediately bear right before reaching the farm buildings. Go over a stile beside the metal gate and turn left and walk down the field keeping the hedge on your left. At the end, go through the gate, turn immediately right and continue to the corner of this field. *This area can be extremely wet after rain.* After the hedge/stream to your right turn left, and follow the direction of the fingerpost (Public Footpath) to the western field boundary angle of the field. Cross a stile which leads onto a bridge, cross the bridge and go over another stile out into the field opposite. Go straight ahead for a short distance and then turn right following the footpath around the field boundary. In the corner of this field, turn left and walk

ahead keeping the fence and hedge on your right. Continue to follow the fence on slightly rising ground past a section with no hedge, until you reach a metal gate. Go through the gate and walk uphill, keeping the woodland to your right, to the top of the rise where you reach a lane.

4. Go over a stile and turn left to follow the metalled lane uphill; there are good views to the right. Ignoring the footpath (another lane) to your right going downhill, continue ahead along this lane. After passing an attractive house on the right, the lane bends to the right and you will have stunning views of the South Downs ahead of you. There is a seat on this corner from which to admire them. The metalled lane now becomes a farm track and in a short distance you pick up the Downs Link path coming in from the left. **To complete walk B, go to section 10.**

5. To complete walk A, go straight ahead downhill on the Downs Link as it winds its way southwards. Ignore the footpath going off to the left at a farm and continue ahead on the track for about 1km/²/₃mile until it becomes a metalled road. Proceed ahead, ignoring all paths to the right, and go over the old railway bridge and carry on along King's Barn Lane, past the treatment works. In about 400m/¹/₄mile, you pass some farm buildings on the left and shortly, as the road bends sharply to the right, go straight ahead onto a track beside a bungalow. Cross a stile on your left and follow the path ahead going down towards the river. Before you reach the stream, turn right onto the footpath that goes along the first field boundary you reach. Follow this path which runs parallel with the stream below you, until you reach a stile. Cross this and carry straight on ignoring the footpath going off to the right until eventually the path goes uphill and divides. Turn right (signpost Public Footpath) and continue to the end of the footpath where it meets the Downs Link once again. Turn left and follow the road round to the turrets at the entrance to Bramber Castle.

If you want to visit the ruins (English Heritage – no charge) or the interesting 11th century St Nicholas church outside the moat, turn left and go uphill into the car park and to the entrance beyond. They are both worth a short visit and also provide an excellent stopping place for a picnic. After your visit to the castle/church, return to the entrance.

6. Turn sharp left immediately in front of the far turret at the entrance road to the castle to go down to the minor road that leads towards the river Adur and Upper Beeding beyond it. Cross the road, turn left and walk ahead into Bramber, pass the lovely 15th century house, St Mary's, which is open to the public, or call in for refreshments, and continue until you reach its car park, the point where the walk turns north for its return leg.

If you wish to take a refreshment break in Upper Beeding, continue along the road about 200m/220yards and two pubs can be found immediately on the other side of the bridge over the River Adur. Return to St Mary's car park to continue the walk.

7. Cross the road, go over a stream and then a stile beside the metal gate ahead of you. Follow this path, a wide grassy track going north, until it reaches the bank of the Adur; turn left onto the river bank and walk a very short distance, go over a stile and turn right to cross the river via an iron bridge. Go over the stile at the far side of the river and carry straight on across a meadow, heading towards the South Downs, with a church and houses on a rise to the right. Cross a stream and continue ahead, keeping the stream on your left, until you reach a wooden walkway/footbridge and a stile. Cross the footbridge/stile, go though a gate into a field and carry straight on to a gate ahead. Go through this onto a track and you now reach a house at the junction with a farm road. Turning left continue on up the gravel track, keeping the dyke on your left. Go forward, passing through an iron gate and on until you reach a stile beside another gate. Cross this stile and continue ahead across a meadow keeping a dyke on the left. Go over two stiles and when the dyke meets a right hand tributary, follow this tributary a short distance until you reach another stile. Cross this and go straight on towards the fingerpost you can see 150m/165yards ahead of you on the raised riverbank. When you reach the riverbank, turn right and walk along the bank until you reach the Downs Link path which crosses the river via an old railway bridge near Stretham Manor. Cross this bridge, where there is a seat for a brief stop, turn right through a gate and walk along the left hand (west) side of the river for about 3km/1^3/$_4$miles until you reach the second bridge where you turn left.

8. Take the path going straight ahead across the field, leaving the river behind you. Go over a stile into the next field and cross this to the gate straight ahead and again take the stile into another field. Follow the hedge on your left around the field boundary and head towards a fingerpost next to a large tree where you turn left and go up the slope towards a gate. Cross over a stile beside it onto a farm track and turn right to follow the direction of the fingerpost along the track until you reach a barn on your right. Here you fork right on a concrete track which leads to the road (B2135) ahead.

9. Turn left along the road and follow the verge a short distance to the Fountain Inn. Cross the road here and take the footpath near the telephone box opposite the Fountain Inn, cross a stile and go straight ahead across a field keeping the hedge on your right hand side. At the corner of the field, cross a stile and go ahead with a post and rail fence on your left; continue past two fields, crossing two small footbridges out onto a minor road. *If you want to see Ashurst church, which has connections with Sir Laurence Olivier, turn right; the church is a very short distance along on your right.* Otherwise, turn left along the minor road to go slightly uphill to a triangle of grass in the middle of the road where you go straight ahead into School Lane. Follow this road a short distance round the corner back to the car park.

Walk B – (via Henfield) (17^1/$_2$km/11miles)

Follow the directions from Ashurst to the Downs Link path - sections 1-4 in Walk A.

10. When you reach the Downs Link, which joins the track from the left where there is a pair of metal farm gates, turn left beside these gates and go through the wooden gate on the left onto the gravel farm track - the Downs Link. Follow this track down the hill towards the River Adur, bearing left at the foot of the slope where you pick up the line of the old railway. Ignore the paths to the right and continue along this track to the old railway bridge close to Stretham Manor where there is a seat for a short stop. *Should you wish to shorten your walk, turn left here and walk along the left hand (west) side of the river until you reach the second bridge where you turn left. Now follow the directions in sections 8 and 9 to return to the car park. See sketch map.*

11. Cross the river and turn right to go over a stile beside a metal gate and walk ahead along the river bank for about 300m/330yards. Just before you reach the pylon taking transmission cables across the river, turn left and take the footpath just below the river bank to emerge into a field. Continue ahead keeping the hedge on your left and pass under the cables. At the end of the hedge continue ahead on the footpath, now a tarmac drive coming from Stretham Manor, and follow this past Stretham Farm House. Ignore another drive (Public Footpath) going off right, and shortly after turn left onto a footpath to go ahead across farmland until you reach a small brick bridge. Cross this bridge and turn right.

12. Continue straight on, staying on the left bank of the stream and shortly afterwards, you reach a small weir. Ignoring the stile ahead, turn left and walk along the footpath by a hedge to the corner of the field. Cross a stile by a gate, and walk over a tiny muddy stream. This could be difficult in wet conditions, but is normally easily passable. Skirt along the edge of two more meadows, keeping the hedges on your right. Go through a wooden five-bar gate and keep straight ahead, either on the edge of the meadow, or just to the right of the hedge along a track with trees either side of you. This track seems to peter out towards the end of the meadow, so you will have to go through into the field again. Cross a stile, and you will find a house and modern barn on your right. Take the path which forks to the right, passing through a five-bar gate, and in front of a house. Ahead of you are two more wooden five-bar gates – go through the right hand one, and follow a very pretty grassy track between high hedges, up a slight incline. After a few minutes, two footpaths are signed, both veering to the left. Take the right of these and continue on along a very beautiful wide sunken trackway with trees on both sides eventually passing ponds to your left and right. As the trees begin to thin out, you will pass another pond on your right. Continue to a tarmac lane, turn right and follow this lane a short distance until you reach the main Henfield to Upper Beeding road (A2037), where there is a sign saying Broadmere Common.

13. Cross carefully over the main road onto a wide verge, turn left and you will leave the roadside and follow a path up a hill and through trees, until you meet another path. Turn right here, almost doubling back on yourself, and continue to the top of the hill where the path levels out. Leaving the trees behind, veer to the left and follow the path along the ridge, known as The Lydds. Ignore the left hand turn, and continue along the path, where there are wonderful views across to the South Downs to your right. There are several benches placed at intervals along this path, providing a good opportunity to stop for refreshments. Continue ahead, ignoring the next path to the left, and follow the path as it goes slightly downhill. Ignore a path to the right, but follow the track round to the left passing a modern house, then turn sharp left round the side of the house and uphill again on a concreted path to the main road (A281) ahead. You will find yourself facing Henfield Cricket Club, founded in 1771.

14. Cross over the road, skirt to the right of the cricket field, to go past the clubhouse to a tarmac lane. Turn left to go along the lane/drive. Just before you reach houses on your right, turn left onto the footpath/access road to Pigeon Croft. When the drive turns right into the house, continue ahead into woods and go straight on ignoring other paths until you emerge at a tarmac lane. Turn left onto the lane and carry on passing a variety of cottages on the right. Where the lane veers to the left keep straight ahead onto a gravelled path, passing Lavender Cottage which was once the centre of a thriving violet-growing industry. Continue along the narrow pathway, one of many in Henfield where they are known as 'twittens', turning right at Henfield High Street where refreshments are available. Continue along the High Street and immediately beyond the second set of traffic lights, cross the road and turn left along Church Street.

15. Walk past Craggits Lane and Chestnut Way on your left, and keep to the left of the small triangle of grass passing 'the Cat House' on your right, a little thatched cottage with motifs of a cat with a canary in its claws all around the walls. Continue along Church Terrace into the churchyard of St. Peter's parish church which, with its square tower and knapped flint walls, is well worth a visit. Leaving by the front entrance to the church, turn right and follow the road to Church Street, to cross straight over into Sobell Court. *Do not go through the lych gate onto the cemetery path.* Go straight ahead, keeping the houses on your right, to a footpath at the end of the houses and continue ahead on the tarmac path until you reach a tarmac road. Turn left staying on the pavement and keeping the Youth Centre building and grounds to your left, go straight ahead on a tarmac path, with the playing fields on your left. At the junction with cross paths continue ahead along the left hand field boundary to the corner by a copse where you turn right to follow a row of trees and a ditch on your left. Halfway down the field, cross over the ditch into the next field on your left, so that the culvert is now on your right and continue down the field to a fingerpost. Do look at the views of St Hugh's Charterhouse Monastery near Cowfold on the skyline ahead. Turn left following the path so that the field is now on your left. When you reach the end of the field, turn right at the fingerpost and keeping the hedge on your left continue to another fingerpost by a gate on your left hand side. When you reach it, turn left through a gate onto the Downs Link bridleway and go straight across onto a footpath opposite.

16. Follow the footpath ahead between the hedge on your left and fence on your right. At the end of the field, continue ahead to a gravelled farm road; turn left and go slightly downhill. Pass through a metal gate and continue ahead on this wide track through a second gate and follow it uphill. At the Y-junction turn right and follow the gravelled track until it divides beside a barn on your left. Take the right fork and after a short distance at a second fork, keep left to pass Lashmans Hall. Go down a narrow path to the right of the garage of Neaves Cottage and over three stiles to reach the river bank, where you turn left. There are lovely views across the water meadows and often lots of swans and other birds along this part of the river and in the meadows beside it. Continue along the river bank for about 500m/550yards, crossing a stile if the gate isn't open, and then turn right to cross the river at next footbridge. **From here follow the directions in sections 8 and 9 to return to the car park.**

24 Sussex Downland Glory – Clayton, Ditchling Beacon, Wolstonbury Hill and Pyecombe

Ray's walk

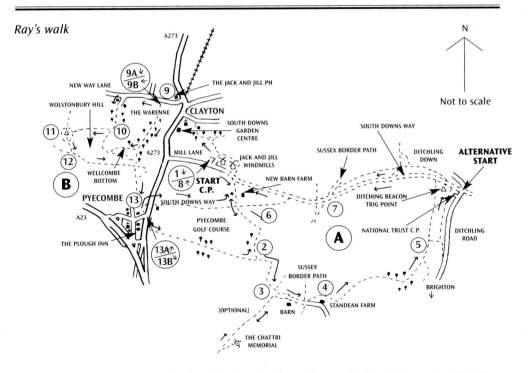

Length: A figure of eight walk of 16³/₄km/10¹/₂miles with a walk, Circuit A, east to Ditchling Beacon of 8¹/₂km/5¹/₄miles with a 1¹/₂km/1mile detour to the Chattri Memorial (sections 1-7) and another, Circuit B, west to Wolstonbury Hill and Pyecombe of 8¹/₄km/5miles using the longer alternative options (sections 9A and 13B). The shorter options (sections 9B and 13A) reduce the length to 6¹/₂km/4miles. Please see sketch map.

Maps: OS Landranger 198; Explorer 122.

Start: GR 303134 Jack and Jill car park on the South Downs, just south of Clayton Village. From the A23 London to Brighton road, turn onto the A273 towards Hassocks and turn into Mill Lane. The car park is on the left.

Alternative start: In summer it is possible to get to the point where the South Downs Way meets Ditchling Road via an open topped bus from Brighton seafront. This would allow you to complete either the whole walk (start at section 6) or just Circuit A via the Jack and Jill windmills (sections 6 and 1-5).

Transport: Bus services from Crawley, Brighton, Burgess Hill and Hassocks travel along the A273 and will stop at the end of Mill Lane leading up to the Jack and Jill windmills, a walk of approximately 800m/½mile.

Refreshments: the Jack and Jill PH, Clayton; the Plough Inn, Pyecombe; cold drinks/ice creams available from van at Ditchling Beacon NT car park; South Downs Garden Centre situated on the A273 half way between Clayton Village and Stonepound crossroads – 1½km/1mile north of Mill Lane.

Introduction: This wonderful walk is mainly on open downland/farmland with extensive views, some of which are quite exceptional. While it is a fairly hilly walk with one steep descent and one steep ascent, there is a great deal of opportunity to see many wild flowers/grasses and different varieties of butterflies. The walk passes through two small downland villages, with churches that are well worth visiting as is the Jill windmill (open to the public on Sundays in the summer, when teas are also available). Railway enthusiasts will enjoy the view of the entrance to Clayton tunnel, built in 1841.

THE WALK

Circuit A (via Ditchling Beacon)

1. Leaving the car park at the entrance, turn left (east) up the gravel road and in about 200m/220yards, at the first junction, bear right continuing on the gravel road. To the right are fine views of Wolstonbury Hill, Newtimber Hill and Chanctonbury Ring. Passing through New Barn Farm, take the green track straight ahead through the gate. In 55m/60yards at cross paths, go straight ahead (south) on a bridleway skirting Pyecombe golf course on the right. This path drops down into Rag Bottom before rising past a small copse into open farmland. Pangdean Holt can be seen straight ahead.

2. Continue ahead for a short distance to meet a waymarker post on a cross path. Turn left here up a slight rise towards a line of trees on the skyline. Pass through the gate turning right; look back for views of the windmills and the distant North Downs. The path runs downhill between a fence and trees for about 200m/220yards before turning left through another gate. This brings you into an open field/downland. The path is not defined, so follow the hedgerow on the right the short distance to the top of the rise. At this point you meet a cross path which is the Sussex Border Path.

If you have plenty of time, a detour from the route can be made here to visit the Chattri Memorial which was built to commemorate the Indian soldiers who fought in the First World War. Some 12,000 came to be treated at Brighton and Hove and 53 were cremated here. To reach it, turn right through the gate and follow the Sussex Border Path (south) for about 800m/¹/₂mile. The Memorial is just below the path on the left-hand side. Return by the same route.

3. Cross the Sussex Border Path and continue straight ahead following the fence to a field gate at the bottom of the field. Go through the gate and follow the chalk farm track down the hill past a brick barn on the right towards Standean Farm. Pass a cattle enclosure on the right and go through the next farm gate which is at the end of the cattle enclosure. *(Do not continue ahead to the farm/cottages because it is almost impossible to find the original path.)* Bear immediately left and go through another farm gate onto a rising path that skirts around the farm complex. This path is marked with a special circular sign and is an official detour around Standean Farm. After passing through a further farm gate into an open field, continue along the green farm track towards the left hand end of a group of trees ahead. Standean and New Barn farms can be seen on the right, with a distant view of the outskirts of Brighton.

4. The track continues to bear left, down the slope to the valley floor, where it joins another bridleway. Keeping left, follow this track along the sunken valley (north east). After approximately 200m/220yards, there is a farm gate and a walking gate in the fence on the right leading into a sloping field. Pass through this gate, turn left to follow the fence line up the slowly rising valley between the two wooded areas. At the head of this long field, pass through a gate and go round a group of small trees. Keeping to the floor of this shallow valley, climb to the end of the field where you will meet a path from the right by the farm gate. Here is an ancient directional post, familiar to this area, with the names of various destinations on it. Go through the gate and climb the path between fences up Heathy Brow. Don't forget to stop and look back to take in the extensive views across the fields towards Patcham windmill at the back of Brighton, the sea and Worthing. On a really clear day, you should be able to see the Isle of Wight.

5. Near the top of the hill there is a choice of two paths leading directly to the brow of the South Downs at Ditchling Beacon – either go straight ahead through a farm gate and follow the path for about 500m/550yards or alternatively turn right through the small gate beside the farm gate. Although less used, this latter is the route I would recommend. Follow the green track for about 100m/110yards and you come to a T-junction (waymarker post). Turn left here along a footpath that tends to be overgrown, between two fields. The effort is worth it because to the right are magnificent views of the rolling downland east towards Lewes, and beyond to Firle Beacon. On a clear day you can see the rise of Seaford Head on the coast through the gap formed by the Ouse valley. Although the path is not well defined, continue straight ahead (north) and you will come to a gate which leads you onto the open downland at Ditchling Beacon. On your left is the OS triangulation stone (trig point) marking the top of the Beacon, the highest point on the South Downs at 248m/780feet above sea level. Just ahead is the edge of the South Downs escarpment and the absolutely magnificent views over the

Sussex Weald towards the Mid Sussex ridge. If you look carefully, you will also be able to pick out two or three windmills in the valley below, evidence of some of the rural industry that took place in this area in days gone by.

This is a good point to stop for a drink and short rest. If you need to cool down turn right along the main path and go through a gate. In about 100m/110yards you will come to the National Trust car park. Here on most days during the year you will find a local ice cream van.

6. To continue from Ditchling Beacon trig point, head west along the top of the Downs back to the Jack and Jill windmills. This can be done by walking along the South Downs Way (SDW) at the crest of the Downs to where it meets the Sussex Border Path (about 1¹/₂km/1 mile). However I would strongly recommend that when starting this section of the walk, after leaving the gate, you look for the grassy track just to the right of the main chalk path. This path follows the outline of the edge of the escarpment of the Downs and provides excellent views of ancient field patterns and the Sussex villages of Ditchling and Keymer below. Ahead can be seen Wolstonbury Hill, on circuit B of the walk, Chanctonbury Ring and the distant Black Down on the Surrey/Sussex border. Continuing in a westerly direction along this path, you come to a fenced off area. Go through the gate into the 'access land' of Ditchling Down, which in the summer abounds with wild flowers and grasses together with numerous butterflies. A little further on, climb over a stile into the area of gorse bushes and going ahead slightly to the right, walk around a slight headland and a deep valley opens up. Keep to the higher ground following either of the upper paths and continue across the meadow, parallel to the fence on the left. Pass the first access gate on the left and continue on past some gorse bushes on the right and you come to another ancient marker post. This is where the Sussex Border Path (the section between East and West Sussex) makes its way up the side of the Downs from the Weald below. Go left through the gate onto the main chalk path and turn right through another gate.

7. Continue straight ahead (west) following the chalk path, the SDW. On the left are views of Brighton and the sea, whilst ahead Pyecombe village can be seen nestling at the foot of Newtimber Hill. After passing through another gate, the path descends slowly with the arms of the Jack and Jill windmills peering over the edge of the horizon ahead of you. In about 400m/¹/₄mile you pass the point where a branch of the SDW turns left. Continue ahead past the next left turn. About 200m/220yards past this second junction, take the small footpath on the right which leads round the windmills out onto the open downland on the north side of the car park where you started the walk. From here you can see below the ancient village of Clayton. For those doing just Circuit A, your journey can end here; equally well you can use this for a lunchtime picnic stop. However, for those undertaking the complete figure of eight walk, as there is an alternative spot to picnic and the option of a pub little further along the route, it would be better to continue.

Circuit B (via Wolstonbury Hill and Pyecombe)

8. To continue the figure of eight walk or start the westerly circuit to Wolstonbury Hill, leave the north end of the car park and head down the side of the hill towards the church, picking up the well-worn chalk track a little lower down. This track descends steeply through a meadow to a gate, which leads the track through a small copse down to the road (Underhill Lane) at the bottom of the hill. *Please note that this section of the path can be very slippery in wet weather.* Turning left, walk the short distance along the lane to Clayton church, past an interesting building on the left. The church, with its unusual lych gate and fine medieval wall paintings is well worth a visit. This is another good stop for a lunch break. For those who have brought a picnic, this can be taken in the sports ground immediately opposite the church where there are plenty of seats. To continue the route (and reach the pub), go to the end of the lane and cross the very busy A273 road with care. Turn right and cross the railway bridge; the pub is on the corner of the lane. *As you cross the railway bridge, do stop and look at the impressive, castle-like entrance to the 2km/1¼mile Clayton Tunnel, scene of a major collision in 1861 when 25 people were killed and 176 injured. This edifice goes back to the original construction of the London, Brighton and South Coast Railway and was built to impress the investors in this railway when one of the last barriers on the line from London to Brighton was conquered. The little bungalow building between the turrets was added later for the linesman of this section of the railway.*

9. From the public house (south side) turn right along New Way Lane, a quiet country byway, towards Wolstonbury Hill. There are two routes that can be taken to reach the summit of this hill, both providing different aspects of the ancient Sussex countryside. Both are described below:

Option A: After about 150m/165yards, there is a chalky bridleway on the left which is the first route, but note that path tends to be rather muddy and slippery in wet weather. Taking this route, the path climbs fairly steeply up the hill through ancient medieval woodlands. After about 800m/¹⁄₂mile, look carefully for a fingerpost and narrow footpath on the right. This path drops down fairly sharply into the depths of the woods and emerges onto a sandy path at the base of the hill. Turn right and follow this sandy and chalky path around the base of the hill passing a small downland dewpond on the left. It is suggested that this was the site of an ancient Saxon village. Continuing on this chalky path around Wellcombe Bottom, as you reach the top of the rise keep a careful eye for a stile on the left in a gap in the vegetation. *(If you reach a gate on your left, you will have gone past the stile.)* Climb over this stile into a grassed area that was once a small ancient chalk pit.

Option B: For this easier alternative route, continue along the road past the chalky bridleway. Go past the road junction on the right and continue ahead over a small rise. In about 250/300yards, turn left onto a footpath at the entrance to The Warenne. Passing a derelict barn on the right, go through Avens Gate to the right of the house into the woods where the chalk path climbs steadily through the woods for a short distance to a corner where there is a nice view back across Wellcombe Bottom.

Do not take the footpath on your left into a field but continue for a little further and the path divides. Now take the path (a bridleway) to the left which leads around Wellcombe Bottom and in about 100m/110yards brings you to a partially hidden stile on the right. Climb over this stile into a grassed area that was once an ancient chalk pit.

10. Now complete the climb for either option, by heading for the direction post immediately ahead, between two trees on the rim of the excavations. This small area is a haven for wild flowers and numerous species of butterflies and moths. On reaching the direction post turn left and start the climb to the summit of Wolstonbury Hill. Follow the grass path to the top of the hill; the path climbs steadily to a stile and once beyond the stile, it then steepens up the last section of about 200m/220yards. There is plenty of reason to stop for short rests as the views behind you are stunning and there is a great variety of wild plants/grasses and butterflies to be found. On reaching the summit, you have arrived at an ancient Iron Age hill fort, the outer mounds of which are clearly visible, with an old OS triangulation point in the centre. There are quite remarkable views from the top of the hill and it is well worth allowing some time to walk around the northern (right hand) perimeter of the hill fort. To the east can be seen the Jack and Jill windmills, Ditchling Beacon and the mid Sussex ridge towards Heathfield. To the north are Hassocks, Hurstpierpoint and the Sussex Weald towards Crawley; to the northwest, the North Downs and Black Down; to the west, Devil's Dyke, Chanctonbury Ring and the whole vista of the South Downs heading west. To the south, through a gap in the Downs, you can see Brighton and the English Channel. Surely the effort in getting to the top is truly rewarded with these magnificent views!

11. The walk continues as you start the homeward run. Crossing the top of the hill past the triangulation point to the western side, look for the path on the edge of the outer ditch/defence mound of the fort which can be quite difficult to find in high summer. Turn left here and follow the path along the outer mound around the hilltop. This area too abounds with wild flowers, grasses and butterflies. Shortly after the Clayton windmills come back into view, the path divides. Turn right and follow the green track (south) to a boundary fence. On passing through the fence, turn left on the chalky farm track. *Should you be unable to find the narrow path on the edge of the mound you can continue westwards down the steep side of the hill, going over a stile until you meet a chalky farm track (bridleway). Turn left and follow this rising track to the top of the hill where you will meet the path from the hill fort.*

12. Follow this chalk and grass track along the ridge of the Downs through a gate downhill for about 800m/¹/₂mile to another gate. Passing through this gate, turn right and you are at a crossroads of chalk paths. Go ahead on a bridleway marked with a waymarked post which leads you downhill about 800m/¹/₂mile into the attractive village of Pyecombe. At the crossroads in the village, by turning right there is the opportunity to visit a lovely Norman church. The entrance to the church boasts a very rare 'tapsel gate', one of only a few left in Sussex.

13. From the crossroads, turn left down Church Lane, bringing you back on the South Downs Way and in 100m/110yards you reach the busy A273 road from which there are two options for the return to the car park.

Option A: For the shorter route, turn left up the hill following the footpath behind a hedge for about 150m/165yards. At this point, cross the busy main road into the entrance of the Pyecombe golf gourse. As you climb the entrance drive, the path can be seen ahead to the left. Follow this flinty track uphill through the golf course for about 1¹/₂km/1mile, where it passes through a gate and a little further on you reach cross paths. Turn left here and retrace your steps of the very first section of the walk through New Barn Farm and then, following the gravel road, bear left back down the hill to the car park.

Option B: For the longer and more attractive route, turn right when reaching the A273 and immediately cross the road carefully to enter the field opposite by the gate/stile. Turn right and walk parallel with the road for about 100m/110yards. Pass through a gate and turn left up the hill between bushes and a fence. Proceed straight ahead uphill between two fields until you come to a copse at the brow of the hill. Go through the gate into the copse and continue ahead. As you leave the copse you will come out onto a golf course. Please take care here. Continue straight ahead to a gate and pass through onto open farmland. Go forward until you reach a marker post on the right. Turn left and follow this bridleway down into Rag Bottom and along beside the golf course on your left. Climbing steadily you will come to a cross path. Go straight ahead and pass through New Barn Farm. Continue on this gravel road, bearing left at the next junction and you will very shortly return to the car park where the walk started.

For those in need of refreshment there is a tea/coffee shop at the South Downs Garden Centre on the A273. Leaving the car park, at the bottom of the access road, turn right onto A273. Proceed to the bottom of the hill and bear left over the railway bridge past the 'Jack and Jill' public house. The garden centre is about 800m/¹/₂mile further along on the right hand side of the road.

25 Birds, boats and barges - Chichester, Fishbourne, Dell Quay and West Itchenor

Monica's walk

Length: a figure of eight walk centred on Chichester Marina of 24³/₄km/15¹/₂miles, with a circular walk towards Chichester, circuit A, of 12¹/₂km/8miles (sections 1-8) and another to West Itchenor, circuit B, of 9km/5¹/₂miles (sections 9-11, 14 and 15) with an optional loop beyond of 2³/₄km/1³/₄miles (sections 12 and 13).

Maps: OS Landranger 197; Explorer 120.

Start: GR 836010 car park on the approach road to Chichester Marina.
From the A27 Chichester bypass take the A286 signed to Birdham, West Itchenor and The Witterings. After 3km/2miles turn right onto the approach road (beware speed bumps). The car park is on the right before you reach the buildings and the boats.

Alternative start: GR 859043 Chichester railway station. Start circuit A or the whole walk at section 3.

Transport: Chichester station is served by SW Trains and Southern; the bus station is very close by. West Itchenor can be reached by bus from Havant, Bosham and Chichester (start at section 12).

Refreshments: the Waterside Inn and a selection of pubs, restaurants and cafés, Chichester; the Crown and Anchor PH, Dell Quay; the Ship PH at West Itchenor; café at Chichester Marina.

Introduction: Chichester harbour is one of my favourite places at all times of the year. While very busy in summer with boats of all sizes enjoying the facilities, it has a special magic in winter and this walk allows you to see many aspects of the area. Bird life is especially good when there are waders in profusion as well as geese, eider duck and red breasted merganser seen on the harbour, while in spring and summer bushes beside the old Chichester canal are full of small birds nesting, and you may be lucky enough to see kingfishers!

THE WALK

Circuit A (via Chichester) 12¹⁄₂km/8miles

Not to scale

1. Leave the car park and turn left and head back via the exit road towards the A286; follow it along keeping the old canal on your right, until the road gently curves away to your left. Keep straight on (on grass) with the hedge and canal on your right until you reach the main road. Cross the road, taking great care, to pick up the footpath almost opposite along the right hand bank of the old canal and continue along the path until you reach another road (B2201). Cross carefully and carry on along the towpath straight ahead again. Eventually as the canal bends to the left (where there is a seat and a convenient place to stop for a break), follow the footpath straight ahead onto the pavement on the busy road ahead. Turn left and stay on the pavement for a short distance until you come to a sign 'Public Footpath and Chichester' on your left, as well as a cycle track sign. Turn left on the footpath and cross the canal on the bridge ahead.

120

2. Turn right on the towpath and continue northwards, now keeping the canal on your right, with a lovely view of Chichester Cathedral ahead of you. Ignore the one path that goes off to the left after some distance (marked Footpath) and continue on along the towpath until you reach a bridge which carries the A27. Go underneath it and keep forward beside the canal. When you meet the tarmac by Poyntz Bridge, carry straight on ahead, avoiding deviating off down the road on your left. (This bridge was moved here from its original location in Hunston and is the only remaining example of a swing bridge on the canal). Do have a look at the board about the Chichester canal on your right and then follow the towpath round to the left where it reaches the Chichester Canal Basin. Continue past a number of seats beside the water and the Waterside Inn on your left hand side. Turn left immediately beyond the Waterside Inn which brings you up onto a busy road (A286). Cross the road, turn right and walk up to Chichester station, crossing the railway line either on the road or via the bridge if the level crossing gates are closed.

3. Turn left into the station forecourt and follow the signs for the South Coast Cycle Route (SCCR) to Fishbourne and Bosham, which bears right in front of a building and then shortly afterwards goes left. Follow this path, keeping the multi-storey car park on your right and continue on, passing under the road (A259) to follow the signs towards the main building of Chichester College ahead of you, walking diagonally right across the grass. When you reach the College turn right and follow the path again as it crosses a small bridge and finally emerges onto a road (Westgate). Turn left here and walk along the road, passing West Sussex County Council Offices on your left until you reach a mini roundabout. Go straight across this and continue straight ahead (still Westgate) using the pavement on the right hand side of the road. As you reach the end of the road turn right to face the entrance to Bishop Luff school where you rejoin the SCCR (now signed for Lavant) which goes off in the left hand corner on a tarmac path, keeping the school buildings on your right.

4. Follow this cycle track until you reach a crossing footpath. Turn left and walk across the field ahead of you on the narrow path which lies between the hedge and the barbed wire fence on your left. This path crosses a narrow metal footbridge into the adjacent field. Continue on with the hedge now on your left until you reach a stile in the fence ahead. Cross the stile and continue to the gate in the left hand corner of the next field close to a mobile phone mast. The path now turns sharply left to go between a ditch on the right and young trees on your left. This is a noisy part of the walk as the A27 is very close by. Eventually the path emerges onto a road where you turn right to walk under the A27 and continue briefly along the right hand verge until you can cross the road to a footpath opposite. Follow this path ahead and cross the railway line with a high stile on either side of the track. After the second stile turn right and go ahead to a stile in the fence. Go over this and turn left along the tarmac track. The buildings on your right are the Fishbourne Roman Palace Museum. Continue ahead when the track bears left and go through a gate. Cross the road and follow the footpath opposite across a stream, eventually coming out onto a field via a kissing gate, with Fishbourne Church ahead of you. Go diagonally left across the field to the stile in the corner, to the right of the kissing gate into the churchyard.

5. Go straight ahead across the field until you reach a stile; cross this, walking diagonally across this field towards the water of Chichester harbour ahead of you. At the end of the field, go up a couple of steps and go straight ahead, ignoring the path to the right. At crossing paths, take the footpath off to your left, going over a stile and continuing across the field ahead of you. (If you want to watch birds you can keep forward on a path around the field following the edge of the water until it joins the other path.)

6. Having crossed the field, continue ahead on a well defined path, keeping the water on your right. Go through a kissing gate and cross another field to a second kissing gate leading into light woodland. Leave the wooded area via a third kissing gate, and continue along the water's edge over a boatyard slipway to reach a tarmac road at Dell Quay opposite the Crown and Anchor pub.

7. Turn left here and carry on up the road until you reach a footpath sign after the last house on your right. Turn onto this path through a squeeze stile in the fence and walk straight on keeping the hedge on your right hand side. Stay on the footpath as it goes right and then turns left, so you're back then with the water on your right hand side. Continue to follow the path round over a small footbridge to your right and at the end of the fields cross a short footbridge into some light woodland with the water now slightly below you on your right. Follow the path until you eventually emerge onto a lane, where you turn right. There's an interesting notice board on your right with information about Salterns Copse through which you have just walked.

8. **If you only wish to complete Circuit A**, go out onto the tarmac, turn left and follow the road/path around the back of the marina until you eventually reach the car park once again. There is a bird hide on your left hand side just before you reach the car park. This is a good spot to look out over the reed beds.

If you wish to continue with the whole walk, go straight ahead with the Marina on your left to cross the entrance. You may need to wait a while for the bridge across the lock gate to be accessible, but there is a seat very close by so you can sit and watch the boats and the birds on the water. Having crossed the marina entrance, go straight on to the road ahead, follow this round to the right until you reach the old canal ahead of you, then turn right and go straight on. On the left hand side of the car park there is a narrow track with the water immediately on your left. Continue on until you reach Salterns Lock and **follow the instructions from section 10.**

Circuit B (via West Itchenor) 9km/5^{1}/$_{2}$miles with an extension of 2^{3}/$_{4}$km/1^{3}/$_{4}$miles

9. From the car park, turn right and walk alongside the old canal, passing Egremont Bridge and pick up the footpath that turns left across the gates of Salterns Lock. There is a Chichester canal information board beside it. There is also a sign on your right, as you start across the lock, for the Salterns Way cycle and wheelchair path.

10. Cross the lock and go along a gravelled hard footpath which divides with a fork across to the right; follow the main track along between two fences to the end and then turn right. This is signposted 'Salterns Way'. This track then brings you out onto a road with a large No Entry sign on your right hand side. Carry on across the road passing the Well House on the corner, the boatyard on your right and then a large pond on your left hand side. Continue along the road, until you come to a footpath sign on a triangle of grass on your right and go along a tarmac road with a sign 'Harbour Meadow, Private Property Footpath Only'. Eventually you reach a footpath sign directing you off to the left beside a field on your left. At the end of the field continue straight on down a now gravelled track with hedges/fences on either side. As you emerge from the fenced area, there is a wonderful view across the harbour. This is a good spot to watch birds as lots of waders seem to like this patch of mud.

11. Continue along the footpath straight ahead with houses on your left hand side and a low mesh fence on your right. Bear left away from the water's edge going between a fence and a wall and at the end of the track, turn right and after a short distance on gravel join the tarmac road. Follow the road round to the left, emerge shortly afterwards onto another road, turn right and go straight on down the concrete road towards Westlands Farm, signposted Salterns Way, rather than deviating left into a field. Turn left at the fingerpost (Public Footpath) ignoring the left hand track marked Salterns Way and take the firm sandy path through the right hand gate passing Westlands Farm on your right. Go straight on, taking the right fork at a Y-junction and follow the line of low transmission cables. Continue on the footpath with the fence now on your left and woodland on your right. At the end of the wood turn left (signposted Public Footpath) onto a tarmac road. Continue along the road until you reach Harbour House on the right hand side after 200m/220yards. Turn right onto the footpath immediately beyond this house walking beside its boundary wall on your right towards the harbour. Turn left along the path with Chichester Harbour on your right until you reach West Itchenor Yacht Club ahead of you and you can see the jetties and slipway on your right. Turn left between the Yacht Club and a wall on your left and continue up the gravel road ahead until you emerge onto a road, opposite the Ship PH.

If you want to take a shorter walk back to the Marina, turn left here and walk up the road (there are no pavements so take great care) until you pass the church. You can then pick up the route of the longer walk at section 14 to get back to the start.

12. Turn right and walk down to the harbour, which makes a nice stop for a picnic as there are a number of benches and a lovely view over the water. With your back to the harbour, turn right and pick up a footpath that goes between a boatyard and houses leaving Jetty House on your right. There are two signs on the wall on your left, one painted and one wooden, as well as a fingerpost. Follow the path until you come out onto hard standing where boats are laid up in winter, and walk straight across this onto the concrete path ahead of you. When the concrete path goes off down to the right, carry straight on, descend almost to the water level and walk along with the harbour on your right. On a clear day as you walk ahead you should get a view of the Spinnaker Tower in Portsmouth away on the horizon.

13. Continue straight on taking the higher path, cross the footbridge and continue forward again with fields on your left and oak trees on your right. Eventually you'll come to a footpath sign, the only one along here. Turn left through a squeeze stile and continue straight ahead with a double fence on your right hand side. Part way along the field cross over the stile on the right hand side and carry straight on along a wide grassy track that eventually becomes a concreted path. When this divides, follow the footpath which goes straight on and just before you reach a barn, cross the stile on your right. Continue ahead with trees on your right and a low knapped flint wall on your left; there are splendid 18th century red brick farm buildings on your left. Go through the gap part way along the wall indicated by the fingerpost and continue straight ahead. When you reach the tarmac track, turn left following the fingerpost, and continue until you reach a road, ignoring the footpath on your right hand side. Turn right and walk carefully along the road passing the parish church of St Nicholas on your left hand side.

14. Shortly after the church take the footpath on the left hand side of the road immediately past Badger Barn. Go over a footbridge and continue straight ahead across a field passing a large barn on your left, into a second field now with a hedge on your right. When you reach the far end of this field, turn right onto the firm sandy track of the Salterns Way. Retracing part of your outward walk, walk past Westlands Farm, through a gate out on to the drive and follow this to reach the road.

15. Go straight along the road, ignoring the footpath to your left which you used on your outward journey and the road to the right signposted Birdham. After about $1^{1}/_{4}$km/$^{3}/_{4}$mile you reach Birdham Church on your right and a triangular green with village pump and a seat beside it, on the left. Cross the green to the right and continue ahead on the road around a narrow left hand bend (no pavement on either side so care needed) and immediately take the left turn into Martins Lane. Walk along this lane passing Broomers Barn on your right, cross a stream and ignore the footpath to your left. Shortly after the road bends to the left, turn right onto a footpath which says 'Private Access Only to Tradewinds' and continue on until you reach Egremont Bridge. Cross the bridge and turn right, to walk along the road until you reach the car park once again.